Praise for
*Reaching Te...*
*in Their Natural* ~~Habitat~~

"Danny Holland's book will give you great insight and practical help to connect with teenagers and understand their culture."

—JIM BURNS, president of HomeWord and author
of *Creating an Intimate Marriage*

"Danny Holland's *Reaching Teens in Their Natural Habitat* is a must-read. In the thirty years that I've taught media literacy, Danny's teaching stands out as effective, profound, and solid. I read every page of his book and plan to read it again and again!"

—DR. TED BAEHR, founder and publisher
of *MovieGuide,* and chairman of the Christian Film and Television Commission

"Danny Holland gives incredible insight into understanding our youth today. I wish this book had been around when we were raising our two sons—it's not only an excellent source for parents, but it's also a must-read for all who want to understand the thinking in our world today from Baby Boomers, Generation Xers, and so on."

—CONGRESSWOMAN JO ANN DAVIS,
Virginia's First District

# REACHING TEENS

## IN THEIR

# NATURAL HABITAT

## A FIELD GUIDE
### FOR SAVVY PARENTS

# DANNY HOLLAND

WATERBROOK
PRESS

REACHING TEENS IN THEIR NATURAL HABITAT
PUBLISHED BY WATERBROOK PRESS
12265 Oracle Boulevard, Suite 200
Colorado Springs, Colorado 80921
*A division of Random House Inc.*

Scripture quotations are taken from the Holy Bible, New International Version®. NIV®. Copyright © 1973, 1978, 1984 by International Bible Society. Used by permission of Zondervan Publishing House. All rights reserved.

Details in some anecdotes and stories have been changed to protect the identities of the persons involved.

ISBN 1-4000-7202-6

Library of Congress Cataloging-in-Publication Data
Holland, Danny, 1969–
    Reaching teens in their natural habitat : a field guide for savvy parents / Danny Holland.— 1st ed.
        p. cm.
    Includes bibliographical references.
    ISBN 1-4000-7202-6
    1. Parent and teenager—United States. 2. Teenagers—United States—Family relationships. I. Title.
    HQ799.15.H65 2006
    306.874—dc22

                                                          2006008613

Printed in the United States of America
2006—First Edition

10 9 8 7 6 5 4 3 2 1

To my mom and dad, Carl and Diane Holland. You trained me in the way I should go before I knew there was a wrong way. You selflessly poured your life into me, encouraging me to embrace my unique purpose. You have lived the pages of this book. Thank you.

To my wife, Amanda Holland. I could not have asked for a better best friend than you. Your limitless encouragement and partnership means more to me than you will ever know. I look forward to putting these words into practice in our home every day alongside my beautiful bride. I love you.

To my sons, Joshua and Caleb. I am so proud of the young men you are becoming. Every day I look forward to walking beside both of you into the great unknown of your future. I am the luckiest dad in the world. I love you guys.

# Contents: The Syllabus

## PART III: PRACTICAL PRINCIPLES
## EVERY PARENT NEEDS TO KNOW

# FOREWORD

I magine a family game show where parents compete for the grand prize by answering questions like (cue the slick host), "What one thing would you want most for your family?"

Without blinking, the parents yell the same thing: "The ability to reach my teens!"

"More than mountains of money?"

"Yes!"

"More than a mansion?"

"Yes!

"More than—"

"Yes! *Yes!* YES!"

The truth is many parents would easily trade in most anything just to have a real relationship with their teens. Far from a fantasy, this truth is too piercing to the heart of every family, too poignant to the state of our union today, and too telling about the destiny of our world tomorrow. Every single person on earth will be impacted by the choices our teens make today. How then do we help guide and influence those all-important choices?

*Reaching Teens in Their Natural Habitat* is a great answer, a tell-all book of tremendous truths for today packaged in simple language. It deals head-on with some of the hottest issues—from understanding a teenager's thinking to the more serious issues of gangs, drugs, and even *(gasp!)* regular sit-down dinners with the family.

Each of us has a stake in the next generation, and we're well familiar with the biblical mandate to "train a child in the way he should go, and when he is old he will not turn from it" (Proverbs 22:6). But what is confusing to many of us is knowing exactly how that works in this day and age. Thank God, Danny Holland's insights have come at just the right time!

—DR. WAYNE CORDEIRO, senior pastor
of New Hope Christian Fellowship
in Honolulu, Hawaii

# ACKNOWLEDGMENTS

Thank you to...

*Jesus Christ.* You never cease to amaze me with infinitely intricate surprises along the road of my life. Thanks for Your lordship, friendship, and leadership. You are so much more than I ever imagined You could be when, years ago, I was first captivated by Your life—and that moving flannel graph. To You be all the glory.

*Pastor Ron and Sandy.* Your leadership and mentorship are absolutely invaluable. Your vision, wisdom, example, passion, and DNA are dripping from this book. The open pages of your lives have served as a vivid testimony of the consistency between all you preach and the way you live. Your family is the loudest message you could preach, and all who've seen your family have seen the truth. Thank you for your leadership, support, and friendship.

*Anonymous students.* To all the young people who have allowed me the privilege of being a part of your life for the past two decades. You have impacted me more than you'll ever know. The knowledge I have gleaned from our countless conversations and the experiences we've walked through together are packed into my life and bleed onto these pages. May your pain and suffering bring healing to thousands.

# INTRODUCTION

You need this book if you have teenagers you are genuinely concerned about. If you have younger children and are wondering about the influences they are encountering, this book will help. If you're a parent, grandparent, foster parent, youth worker, educator, counselor, police officer, or any kind of caregiver, and even if you have a relatively strong relationship with the teens you know, you will find something in this book to help you keep your grip and win more ground in the battle for their minds.

Now, I don't live in your home, and I don't pretend to know what your family has walked through; however, I have a unique purpose for writing this book. For several years I have worked in schools dealing with students from various backgrounds. My work has put me in uncommonly close proximity to students who have severe behavioral issues and destructive habits. Some of these students may even resemble young people you know well. Throughout this book you will hear about, as well as from, many of the teens I work with. Right now, I'd like to tell you about one of them. I was called into my school administrator's office to meet with a parent. As I entered the room, the father of a student greeted me. He was a high-ranking military officer in dress uniform, complete with an array of medals. He was pretty intimidating. He began explaining his struggle with his son's behavior, a student I'd been regularly working with. As tears streamed down his face, he turned to me and said, "Danny, you *have* to reach my son. You are the only one who can. He talks about you day and night."

That day I realized that nobody wants to reach kids more than their own parents do. But why could I be more successful at reaching a young man with whom I spent a few minutes each day than a father with a sincere passion to connect with his son? At that moment I realized, parents who are equipped with the understanding and techniques I use to connect with kids could be far more effective than I. The material in this book is designed to help you do just that.

The strategies and techniques you'll find here are not theories from the pages of great parenting textbooks. Instead, I have successfully used these approaches for nearly two decades in public schools, churches, police cars, and just about every other environment imaginable. I have taught them to pastors in Russia, parents in England, and educators across America who are now successfully reaching young people. These techniques can also work with your teenager.

This book will not just point out problems; it will help you become part of the solution. It is not a cure-all substitute for family counseling or input from other sources of wisdom, but it will help you build stronger relationships and communicate better with your teens. The bottom line is that what you are about to read in this book works. It's worked for me, and it will work for you.

I can't promise you'll like everything you find in these pages. (I personally am constantly challenged by these ideas!) So it might be best if you think of me as your friendly weatherman. Just because I say it might rain on your picnic doesn't mean I created the rain. But there are dynamics in action in every home that you need to be aware of. You may realize that some of those dynamics are producing negative results. And once you understand the techniques I use, you will be able use them with your teen to help turn the weather to your advantage.

This book is a toolbox, and the tools you'll find here are not obscure secrets. They are used every day in the hallways of our schools by drug dealers, gang members, and others. Once you recognize these, you'll see them used on television, on the radio, and by others whose business involves capturing the attention of young people. You will notice these approaches being used to sell products and communicate values and ideas. But you'll also learn how to use these same techniques in a positive way to communicate your values, pass on your traditions, and have an impact on the future of young people around you.

Furthermore, as you see advertisers' various agendas, I believe that your passionate desire to deepen your relationships with the teens in your life will help you be *the* greatest influence in their lives.

So sit back, relax, and begin to think of yourself strategically wielding these new tools like a skilled craftsman, molding your teenagers into the young people they are meant to be.

# Part I

# UNDERSTANDING
# TODAY'S YOUTH

# The American
# Teenager in Its
# Natural Habitat

*The American teenager in its natural habitat.* Does that phrase conjure up images of the Crocodile Hunter wrestling into submission that scaly foreigner who lives in the back bedroom? Or maybe you're envisioning an alien being far too complex to understand. No matter what imagery comes to your mind, the title of this chapter gives the right sense of the situation. Let's hop into our imaginary blimp and take it up for an aerial view.

"Our earth is degenerate these days; there are signs that the world is speedily coming to an end; bribery and corruption are common; children no longer obey their parents; and the end of the world is evidently approaching." Sounds like something out of today's newspaper, doesn't it? Actually these words were found carved on an Assyrian stone tablet dated 2800 BC. Although in some ways young people have been similar for thousands of years, the culture the previous generation refines and leaves for the next does have an impact on that generation. So to really understand today's teens, we need to look at the generations that have gone before them.

## The Generations

Let's take a quick look at the common divisions of generations: the Baby Boomers, Generation X, and the Millennials.

### *Baby Boomers*

It's generally agreed that Boomers comprise those people born between the end of World War II (1945) and 1965. They were the first to carry the label "teenager." They lived through the Cold War with the threat of Soviet nuclear-missile attacks, and the most notable moment in history for this generation was the assassination of President Kennedy. Then the civil rights movement and the Vietnam War began to heat up and became prominent issues for Boomer teens. Family values began to erode due to the hippie/free love movement and the rising popularity of hard drugs. Older Boomers entered the work force and became our modern corporate America. They are product-driven, task-oriented people who have had a tremendous impact on our nation.

### *Generation X*

Typically, an Xer is someone born between 1965 and 1981. The older ones started life during the Vietnam War. They watched adult generations reach new heights when astronauts walked on the moon, and they saw those same generations experience uncommon lows with the resignation of President Nixon.

The cultural trait that had the greatest impact on Xers was the state of the American family. Divorce rates escalated during these years, and Xers paid the price. In addition to their divorce rate, the Boomers' preoccupation with themselves resulted in painful family dynamics. Furthermore, sex and drugs, corporate-ladder climbing, and the women's movement combined to make child rearing a low priority for Boomers. Millions of Xer kids went home each day to empty homes because their Boomer mothers had entered the work force to achieve "self-fulfillment" and to help sustain a lifestyle that fathers alone could not support. It's estimated that in 1982 in the United States alone, 25 percent of Xer kids aged six to twelve were latchkey kids—that's seven million children.[1]

It's been said that what one generation tolerates, the next will embrace, and no words ring more true of sexual experimentation in the seventies and eighties. During this time our nation hit one million teen pregnancies each year, and sexually transmitted diseases spread like wildfire, the most famous of which remains incurable—AIDS.[2]

But not all news about the Boomers as adults and their legacy is bad news. After all, technology exploded through developments in the space program, medicine, and computers, to name a few. Knowledge grew rapidly, and Xers and Millennials are profiting from the Boomers' hard work.

## Millennials

Born between 1982 and the present, during a season of unprecedented prosperity, Millennials were the first generation without a cause in modern history. But when the Twin Towers at the World Trade Center came down on September 11, 2001, this generation found its cause. Innocence was lost and evil was exposed. Shaken to the core by this atrocity, Millennials became consumed with living in harmony with others.

The events of 9/11 forced many American schools to suddenly realize that their crisis plans may have been adequate for dealing with threats from students *within* their buildings, but they had no solution for dealing with threats from *outside* their buildings, due to the political climate of the world at large.

As a result, Millennials actually like change. In fact, they regard change as a normal part of everyday life; it's as natural to them as water is to fish. Millennial kids have grown up with daily access to more technology than any generation before them, and the first generation of Internet-savvy children has emerged. Parents of young people today are the first generation to have to educate their children about online threats, such as identity theft, music piracy, and child predators.

These Internet-savvy kids enjoy a world without boundaries. They chat with kids around the globe and have relationships without geographical limitations. Younger members of this generation have never lived during a time when they could not immediately chat with someone in China, Russia, or Australia. They are plugged in and online. And by the time Millennials turn five, they have already watched thousands of hours of television.

Boomers and Generation Xers embraced tolerance and political correctness, so relativity is alive and well with Millennials. In fact, the absence of absolute truth and an agreed upon standard of right and wrong leaves this young generation without the most basic tool for avoiding pitfalls in life. Consider the conversation I had with one Millennial. She was telling me that she is avoiding drugs even though most of her friends abuse drugs regularly in front of her. I asked, "Are these people your friends?"

She said, "Yes."

"Do you think watching your friends destroy their lives without doing anything to help them is okay?" I asked.

Confidently, as if she had studied all night for this response, she answered, "I know what drugs do to someone's life. That's why I choose not to take them. They are wrong for me. But if other people choose to take them, that's their choice. I don't think drugs are wrong for them, and they understand that it's wrong for me."

I paused and said, "Let me ask you something. Is anything wrong for everyone?" Now I saw a deer-in-the-headlights expression on her face. I asked, "What about rape? Is it ever okay to rape someone?"

"No!" she insisted.

"So rape is wrong for you," I continued. "What if rape is not wrong for me? Then rape is okay, right?"

"No," she said again.

"Who determines what is right and wrong for everyone?" I asked.

Catching on she sadly answered, "I don't know."

What an amazing moment! No conversation can better capture the spirit of Millennial life. This generation is seeking truth in a world that brands anyone with absolute values as an enemy of freedom, one small step above terrorists.

## SOCIETAL CHANGES

Today Xers and Millennials are watching their parents experience their childhoods again. They're buying Harley Davidson motorcycles, Hummer H2s, boats, houses, and other toys with the money they have acquired over a lifetime of hard work. But Xers are haunted by the high price they paid for that materialism: it cost them stable homes and strong relationships with their moms and dads. As a result, Generation Xers as parents are celebrating their Millennial children much more than they themselves were celebrated. Many Boomers are quick to notice how society has become much more kid centered.

For example, we now see malls with three types of rest rooms—one for men, one for women, and one for families. Fast-food restaurants have play areas, and housing developments have miniature golf courses and water parks instead of traditional golf courses. Although most Boomers will say that cruise ships are for later in life, advertisers are trying to attract young families.

Gen Xers are making their mark in the work force. More than one-third are opting for nontraditional work. In other words, one out of three workers does not work Monday through Friday, forty hours per week. Instead they are telecommuting, working Web-based jobs, job sharing, and so on.

Also unique is the sociologists' expectation that Generation Xers and Millennials will have between six and eight careers in their lifetimes. Many of today's parents grew up watching their fathers and mothers make tremendous sacrifices out of loyalty to their companies, and some of these parents came up empty for the sacrifice.

Their sons and daughters are unwilling to repeat the experience, and corporate America has been quick to respond to these generational trends. A couple of years ago, Silicon Valley dotcom corporations began seeing that the most creative graduates from leading universities were seeking not jobs but locations that supported their lifestyles. Generation Xers and the oldest Millennials are moving to areas that support their interests and values rather than just their careers. This is one reason why big corporations are decentralizing from big cities and traditional locations and placing their businesses in areas where top employees want to live and raise their families.

Another insight that is vital to understanding how they think is the realization that both Xers and Millennials have grown up seeing institutions in a negative light. Again, many Xers watched their parents sacrifice everything for the companies they worked for only to be rewarded with layoffs. They also watched churches and ministries crumble due to the hidden sin of their leaders. They watched their parents ignore their commitment to each other and divorce. They got to watch the president of the United States struggle to define sex. They saw executives at corporations like Enron lie and cheat. And they watched Catholic priests come under fire for committing unthinkable acts with children.

Let's look at the earlier generations, though. Boomers were raised by the Traditionals who trusted their churches because they were churches. They trusted the police because they were the police. As a generation, they trusted authority because it was authority. But then the young Boomers pushed against the boundaries and aggressively rebelled against authority with their war protests, Woodstock, and

## TIPS FROM THE TRENCHES

Certain parents have great success with their teenagers. These children emerge with strong relationships and grow into uncommonly productive young adults. The following comments are from interviews and surveys I conducted with people who can help you successfully connect with your teen.

Dr. Steven Staples, EdD, is one of the wisest individuals I've met. A father and the superintendent of schools for the York County School Division in Virginia, he has navigated teenage years with excellent results. Dr. Ted Baehr is an award-winning producer, writer, director, scholar, good friend, and tremendous parent. An expert on the movie industry, he analyzes media for families on Movieguide.org. Carl Holland is my father and one of the greatest influences in my life. He helped my sister and me through our teen years, and he remains one of my best friends. Ron and Sandy Johnson have four sons, and I can't name parents who have been more successful in providing their boys with foundational values that have launched them toward their unique purposes. Ron is an international entrepreneur, pastor, mentor, friend, and invaluable member of the board of directors of Parent and Teen Universities Inc. (P-T-U.org). Bob Waliszewski is an author and one of the nation's leading youth-culture experts. His weekly *Plugged In Movie Reviews* is heard on three hundred U.S. radio stations, and he has raised two leaders with a powerful sense of purpose.

*What made the difference in your home?*

S. Staples: (1) We ate dinner together almost every night, with no TV or radio on to distract us. The time encouraged communication and shared values as we discussed problems or just everyday events; (2) we attended church together. The time was an important one for all of us to reflect on ethics, morals, values, and something "bigger than all of us" in life; (3) we established clear expectations and standards for behavior in our family. We didn't have to punish [our kids] too many times, because everyone knew and understood what would and would not be acceptable. These expectations included what *to* do (work hard in school, treat others with respect) as well as what *not* to do.

T. Baehr: Faith, love, [and] teaching Media-Wise Family.

R. Johnson: First of all, consistency. What we said is what we tried to live. We didn't have a double standard. This is what [parents] do, but you [kids] do something separate.

S. Johnson: Unconditional love, consistency in our lives, consistent discipline, prayer—asking God, *What is it with this kid?* By unconditional love, I mean determining to love them when you hate what they are doing.

B. Waliszewski: I believe the modeling that both Leesa and I have demonstrated down through the years has really made a difference.

free love. So Generation Xers were raised in Boomer homes with a spark of distrust for institutions, and these Xers have passed on that apprehension to their Millennial kids.

## NO EASY ANSWERS

Today's young generation trusts what they experience. With the overflow of information available today, conflicting information is not difficult to find—even among the most reliable sources. If an institution, organization, or individual wants to reach Xers and Millennials, relying on an institutional image will not work. Likewise, if a parent wants to be respected, honored, and obeyed in the home, it will take more than saying, "Because I'm you're parent."

A recently divorced mother with custody of her fifteen-year-old son came to me for help. She said, "Danny, I'm preaching to him that drugs will destroy his life and that he should avoid them. He just isn't listening. Will you talk to him?"

During the time I spent with this teenager, a few things became very clear. First, he was hurting. The pain bottled up inside this young man was just waiting to erupt. Second, his drug use temporarily took away that pain. Sure, when the high wore off, he experienced additional pain. But to a kid who uses drugs to mask pain, tomorrow is not the greatest concern. "How am I going to survive today?" is the only question.

Let me translate what this young man is really saying: "Mom, I hear you, but I can't trust you, because you tore apart our family and you lied to me. Your words can't outweigh what I know from personal experience: I smoke weed and I feel better. Period."

Millennials have trouble trusting not just Mom and Dad but organizations, institutions, and marketing, in general. When a bumper sticker offers a cute slogan we should all live by, this generation simply doesn't buy it. And there are no easy answers, shortcuts, or quick fixes that will help you instantly gain their trust. You will need to invest—your time, your energy, your love—in Millennials you care about. Once the investment is made, though, results will be dramatic. After all, this generation is seeking; nobody wants to trust more than a Millennial. Nobody wants straight answers more than those who have had to wade through endless voices in search of truth.

Acknowledging this reluctance to trust and this desire to trust is the vital first step to understanding the generational values we'll discuss in the next chapter.

# 2

# Generational Values

I cannot tell you how many Boomer parents have said to me, "You have no idea how lazy my teenagers are. They just sit around and do nothing." This observation about Xers and Millennials, although common, is not completely accurate. That's because each generation has different values. When parents or other adults fail to recognize and understand these differences, communication is impaired, and the transfer of vital information and values fails. Therefore, let's look at generational paradigms that cause misunderstanding and miscommunication.

## TRIUMPH VERSUS TOGETHERNESS

Boomers had a clear agenda in the world: they wanted to rule it. The Boomers were all about what they were accomplishing; their jobs gave them their identities. There is no question that the course of history was impacted by the character, values, and work ethic of the Boomer generation. Their drive to triumph resulted in a global environment where advances in technology, medicine, and other industries began taking new ground. But, again, the Boomer family dynamics many young Xers and Millennials grew up with resulted in two generations determined to rule their own individual destinies. For instance, it is not uncommon for a Millennial to think, *I might work at Taco Town for the rest of my life, but I will surround myself with a community of people I want to be with.*

If you think your teenager is lazy, try to take away his community. Take away his cell phone, e-mail, instant messaging, Web page, and other means of communication. You will suddenly see passion.

I could list names of students who do nothing in school—and I mean literally nothing. I have seen students write "Get drunk" as every answer on every test they take. But let the authorities try to administer discipline by removing them from the school environment and see what happens. When up for expulsion, these students will almost always fight it. Why do they fight being removed from an institution that they don't even attempt to participate in? Because they are being removed from their community.

Clearly, Millennials and younger Xers are driven by relationships. Many Boomers and older Xers contemplate how to "get ahead," but younger Xers and Millennials seek ways that we can all "get along."[1] The difference is valuing accomplishments as opposed to valuing social interaction. Despite their apparent lack of drive, the Millennials' primary value is people. They value relationships.

This generational difference is evident in commercials and television programming, and the examples are endless. When I was kid back in the eighties, one of my favorite shows was *The A-Team*. In every thirty-minute episode the A-Team thwarted some catastrophic event. Hannibal always had a plan, and that plan always came together. It was awesome. This story line was common in the Boomer television era. Boomers wanted to see something accomplished, so shows gave them that. And what a contrast to television today.

Most teen programming today is created by Generation Xers for Millennials. *Friends* was one of the most popular television shows of our time. The six main characters were neighbors. Only half of them had careers, but they all lived in huge apartments in New York City. Most of the time they hung out in a coffee shop and discussed life. Period. That's the show. Many Boomers don't find this concept entertaining in the least; nothing is accomplished. Such community-fueled shows offer nothing more than thirty minutes of hanging out. This is the case in most of the TV shows popular among this young generation. *The Real World, Laguna Beach, American Idol, Fear Factor, Blind Date, Who Wants to Marry a Millionaire?* and *Survivor* are other examples of relationally driven entertainment designed for a relationally driven generation.

## ENDS VERSUS MEANS

Closely related to the triumph-versus-togetherness paradigm is the fact that Xers and Millennials are all about the process, while Boomers are concerned about results. Let me give you an example.

When President George W. Bush decided to go to war with Iraq, those opposed to war voiced two main concerns. Many Americans felt that war would drive the price of gasoline up so high that it would cause an economic crisis in our nation. The other concern was for the young people who were likely to be killed or injured.

It was the Boomers who seemed concerned about the "end" side of this issue. Boomer leaders spent countless hours estimating the war's financial impact. The economic consequences were of very little concern to most Xers and Millennials, though. Generation Xers and Millennials opposed to the war seemed to primarily voice the other concern: "What about my friends who could die?" and "How will those boys feel over there? They're my age and not ready to die for their country." MTV even did a documentary on what it's like to be young and ready to go to war. And Xers and Millennials watched video footage of the invasion through the lenses of relationships. The means of the war was more important to them than what ground was conquered that day, or when the war might end, or the economic fallout of the war.

## ME VERSUS WE

Boomers say, "I'm going to do my own thing," while Xers say, "We're doing our own thing." An African proverb states, "It takes a village to raise a child," and Generation X is living that out. Xers and Millennials are saying, "We will succeed," as opposed to, "I will succeed."

Have you noticed, for example, that kids today do everything in groups? They walk in groups, study in groups, read books in groups, chat in chat rooms in groups, and even kill in groups. This last trend has alarmed those who study youth violence. There were fifty-two violent deaths in American schools in 1995—more than in any other year recorded. In 1999, the year of the Columbine High School massacre, there were twenty-five violent deaths. Despite the fact that Xers as students were more violent, there is a huge emphasis on school safety in the Millennial world. That's because almost every school shooter in recent history acted with a partner or a group, so vigilant parents of Millennials find video game–like replications of horrific acts by boy-next-door teenagers in groups as alarming as it gets.

The "we" of the younger generations can be positive or negative. One positive aspect of "we" is the reduction of racial tension in the midst of a growing multicultural environment. There is much less racial tension among our youth than there used to be. Interracial relationships, which were taboo two generations ago, are largely a nonissue now. This is a signature of young people today. American culture can be more aptly described as a stir-fry rather than a melting pot.

I have a good friend who served for thirty years as a police officer in a public school in the Washington DC area. During his time working in the same school, the ethnic makeup of the school changed dramatically. By the time he left the school, eleven languages were spoken in that one building. All of us may not encounter this firsthand in our communities, but our culture at large certainly does.

We are also seeing the Hispanic population passing the African American population in some states, so new dynamics are at work in America. Though tensions have largely lessened, there are still aggressive conflicts between Hispanic and African American young people in many cities, and these conflicts are putting a new face on gang violence and related conflicts. The paradigm at work here is again the importance of the group over the individual.

## FOLLOW THE RULES VERSUS NO BOUNDARIES

Another huge difference between today's young people and their parents is what I call the anything-goes mentality. As I mentioned in the previous chapter, relativity is alive and well among Xers and Millennials. The only thing Millennials consider wrong is telling other people they are wrong. After all, they think the government, religion, society, parents, and friends cannot determine what is right. "That's okay for you, but not me" is the war cry of these kids, and most of us looking on already understand this on an intuitive level.

Now that we have explored a little about four of the major differences between the generations, let's look at some of the messages that our society is bombarding our children with.

# 3

# Voices of Influence

"Mommy and Daddy, we have a show for you! Come in our room!" Remember when your kids were little? You know that The Show is very important and that this expression of their creativity is one of the most memorable moments a parent can experience.

But on this day, entrenched in work, I have to admit that the timing of The Show could have been much better. My wife, Amanda, assured Josh and Caleb that we'd be right there. But deep in thought as I worked in my home office, I simply didn't have time to see The Show.

Josh, the usher with the flashlight, was waiting to seat Mom and Dad on the two Bob the Builder chairs positioned in front of the stage made from beds. With flashlight on and house lights dimmed, our two boys stood outside my office door.

"Danny, turn your head to the right," Amanda whispered. *Turn my head to the right? They were in the hallway to the left, so why would I look to the right where there was only a wall?* But I glanced to the right, and a picture caught my attention. It's a picture of a boy standing on a beach facing the ocean, and it reads: "PRIORITIES. A hundred years from now it will not matter what my bank account was, the sort of house I lived in, or the kind of car I drove… But the world may be different because I was important in the life of a child." I immediately turned my attention to my boys.

Attention is the battlefield where parents and kids win or lose. My heart breaks for parents who seem to constantly be putting out fires in their teens' lives. Many parents often have issues in their lives that demand so much attention they have little left for their kids. And what attention they do have they seem to spend on the consequences of poor choices and destructive decisions made by their sons or daughters. It's obvious that all parents have a limited amount of attention they can devote to their kids. Clearly, the battle is not only for our teens' attention but also for ours. There are some principles I've studied, refined, and applied over the years that I think are important to point out.

## Whatever Has Our Attention Influences Us

Anything that can capture and keep our attention can control us. A man I respect, Dr. Adolph Brown, once told me, all that is necessary to teach someone a concept is to capture his or her attention. Consider, for instance, that advertisers can easily spend more than ten million dollars on a thirty-second commercial. We need to work hard if our voices are to be heard over all the flashy influences competing for our kids' attention. We cannot casually pursue our kids and expect our words to factor strongly in their decision-making process.

But we need to begin by examining the many voices that try to capture *our* attention. If we're consumed with thinking about that promotion at work, that trip to the islands, a new boat, or some other materialistic dream, our attention has been captured. If we find ourselves constantly thinking about a person other than our spouse, we've been captured. By the same token, if our minds are focused on fulfilling our purpose and developing character, it will be reflected in our daily decisions. And our lives reflect it when we're consumed with helping our children avoid regrets, make good choices, and fulfill their purpose in life.

Focus also affects our kids' decisions. For example, I recently had the opportunity to interview a career drug dealer. Actually, it was my responsibility to knock on his door with a warrant for his arrest and take him away from his family of five. At the jail I mentioned that I travel across the country speaking to teenagers, and I asked him, "What one thing would you like to tell them to help them avoid being where you are right now?" He answered, "Tell them to run from drugs when they are young. When I was ten years old, I started muleing [holding and carrying drugs for dealers], because I thought drug dealers were cool. I should have run then. I started dealing crack when I was twelve years old. Now I'm thirty. I've been shot at, I've lost everything, and now I've lost my family. Tell them to run."

So, Mom and Dad, every decision your children or teenagers make begins because something has captured their attention. Show me what they're paying attention to, and I'll show you the key to their behavior. The battle for our children's future is a battle for their attention today. Whoever captures their attention most consistently will win.

Picture a warehouse full of cars. Some are exotic beauties; others are broken-down junkers. But they all have an autopilot feature with a preset destination. Your teen's focus—what grabs his attention—is the key for one of the cars. Unfortunately, all the keys—all the possible points of focus—say *Lamborghini* on them, but only one actually fits the Lamborghini. Thousands of other flashy keys are screaming, "Over here, Kara!" "Sean, Sean. I'm the real Lamborghini!" "Kim, don't listen to them, I'm the only *real* key." Each child is designed for an exhilarating future full of purpose, contentment, vitality, and excitement. As parents, we may not know which key fits the two-hundred-fifty-thousand-dollar beauty, but we can help reduce the influence of the obvious imposters.

Not one of our children would intentionally pick a key to a painful destination. Most of them sincerely believe that the key they choose will take them where they want to go. And they'll choose the key when something captures and keeps their attention. So how does someone destroy a young person's future? It's easy. Capture her attention and distract her.


## Our Attention Determines Our Direction of Travel

What we look at and listen to will affect our desires, and ultimately, the direction of our lives. Consider the work of Dr. Joseph Goebbels, the National Socialist (Nazi) propaganda minister from 1933 to

1945. In his book *So You Want to Be in Pictures?* author Ted Baehr describes Goebbels's effort to destroy Jews, evangelical Christians, handicapped Germans, and other groups of people through mercy killings: "Finally, Goebbels produced a dramatic movie called *I Accuse,* an emotive feature film about a beautiful, intelligent woman who is dying of an incurable disease and begs to be allowed to commit suicide. After the movie was released, a majority of German people said they had changed their minds and now supported mercy killings. After a few more of Goebbels's films about invalids and handicapped people, the German people voted for mass mercy killings."[1]

Movies influenced the ideas and ethics of the German people. Adolf Hitler was keenly aware of the power of images. As historian Paul Johnson writes in *Modern Times,* "Hitler appears always to have approached politics in terms of visual images. Like Lenin and still more like Stalin, he was an outstanding practitioner of the Century's most radical vice: social engineering—the notion that human beings can be shoveled around like concrete. But, in Hitler's case, there was always an artistic dimension to these Satanic schemes. Hitler's artistic approach was absolutely central to his success. [Historians all agree] the Germans were the best-educated nation in the world. To conquer their minds was very difficult. Their hearts, their sensibilities, were easy targets."[2]

## OUR ATTENTION IS OUR INVESTMENT

Whatever we invest our attention in is an investment in our future. Whether we are investing our attention in the form of our gifts, resources, time, energy, or passion, we are investing in and determining our future.

Now if your daughter received a hundred-thousand-dollar gift and you had legal say in how she spent it, you undoubtedly would help her handle it wisely. You know from experience that how she handles that money could make a tremendous difference in her life a decade or two from now.

Is our teens' investment of time any different? If the focus of our teens' attention and their investment of time can make or break their entire adult lives, how much more vigilantly should we guide those investments? After all, if teens are not watching it, listening to it, playing it, or doing it, they probably won't have strong desires to pursue it.

## What Has Our Attention Attracts Our Energy

Imagine lying in bed in the middle of the night. You're sound asleep when suddenly the phone rings. Adrenaline instantly surges through your veins as a million tragic thoughts flood your mind. An emotion-filled voice on the other end tells you that a loved one has been severely injured and is on the way to the hospital. Do you hang up, roll over, and go back to sleep? No. No matter how tired you are, you're infused with new energy because the news has captured your attention.

In fact, it's been said that time is the currency of our planet. We can lose money and make more, but we don't have that luxury with time. Once it's spent, it's gone, and we get no more. I was once told about the home of one of the most successful youth workers in the nation. Her house had a trampoline in the living room. Everything in her life screamed, "I love kids and want to be with them." Evidence of what kept her attention and energy was visible around her, even in the way she decorated her house. I'm not saying we need to drop the family heirlooms off at Goodwill and convert our houses into teen recreation centers, but I do believe in the value of investigating our lives for evidence that our teenagers have our attention and that we are investing our energy in them.

And speaking of energy, let me say it again: your child is *not* lazy. When I hear parents say that about their teen, I know immediately that I am talking to parents who are struggling to determine what has captured their teens' attention. *And whatever your teen is paying attention to as you read this will shape his future.* Read this powerful statement again and keep it in mind for later.

## INCREASED TIME = INCREASED STRENGTH

Next, whatever you look at most will gain strength and eventually be the strongest attraction in your life. Let me give you an example. I used to have a fascination with Jeeps. I loved looking at Jeeps, checking out the modifications Jeep owners made, and even studying the Jeep concept vehicles. I would dream of taking my new Jeep Rubicon top down, wife and kids strapped in, onto the beach and giving its thirty-three-inch B.F. Goodrich Mud Terrain tires a workout as waves crashed around us. You get the picture. The more I dreamed about having a Jeep, the more often Jeeps caught my eye. I noticed every Jeep that passed me even when I was driving on the interstate at seventy-five miles per hour. By allowing Jeeps to repeatedly capture my attention, I unintentionally trained my eye to notice them.

And what captures our attention is not as important as what keeps it. So study and be an expert in whatever keeps your son's or daughter's attention. It might be something educational and positive. It might even give you a clue as to what your son's or daughter's purpose is in life (we'll get into this in chapter 5). It might be a musical instrument, sport, or civic or church activity. And once you find that captivating item or activity, go out of your way to *feed that source of attention.*

While I was growing up, my father was the news director of a popular radio station, but he was laid off when the ownership changed. I was a teenager at the time, and suddenly I became interested in playing the bass guitar. I had a cheap one, but I quickly outgrew it. After nearly twenty months, my father had not found a job. But even though money was tight, he made a huge investment in my future by buying me an eighteen-hundred-dollar instrument and a thousand dollars worth of accessories for Christmas. I understand something today that I didn't know then: my father saw my attention and energy being drawn toward something positive, and he *fed that source of attention.* Even though some might see his purchase as a poor financial decision for a man in his position, he saw my interest as the opportunity of a lifetime. It's been said that the opportunity of a lifetime must be seized during the lifetime of the opportunity, and that is never truer than when it comes to our kids and their interests.

## Recognize and Promote Allies

As the battle for our kids' attention rages, know that you are surrounded by positive voices that can help you shape your kids in healthy ways. Your ally in this war is anyone or anything that helps your teens keep their attention on their primary purpose. And as you focus your attention on your child, you will be training your eye to recognize potential allies, just as I trained my eyes to notice Jeeps. Then, when you recognize these possible allies, invest your resources in them and encourage their presence in your teens' lives.

Here's an example of how this principle can work. Renting a beach house in a small community in North Carolina during the first week of summer break is a tradition for high schoolers in our area. I'm sure it would be no surprise to anyone what typically happens during "Beach Week." With underage drinking and everything that goes with it, the week is completely out of control. As I was thinking about this event, I visited a local high school, where I recognized a senior I knew casually. She was academically successful and exuded inner character and beauty unique for someone her age.

"So you're getting ready to walk," I said. "Are you going to Beach Week?" She sighed, and I noticed a suspicious excitement on her face.

"No. You won't believe what my mother did. She had already planned a mother-daughter shopping trip to New York City for that week. I get to go shopping in Manhattan!"

I smiled and celebrated with her, silently admiring the strategic move these parents had pulled off in order to attract the attention of their daughter. What a wise and timely use of resources. I am personally challenged by parents like these and reminded that young men and ladies of character don't just happen.

## RECOGNIZE AND DETER ENEMIES

There may be influences in the lives of our kids that are not necessarily encouraging them to take drugs, kill people, or commit suicide, but there is still good reason to restrict their potential effect. We have a tremendous influence on how successfully our kids will pursue their purpose and avoid painful regrets. We'll talk more about

---

## SIX THINGS PARENTS CAN DO TO DIRECT THEIR TEENAGER'S ATTENTION

1. Recognize that distractions destroy dreams.
2. Train your kids and teens to guard their own focus. Only your children can protect themselves.
3. Control the type of music, media, and teen entertainment that your kids are exposed to.
4. Starve wrong relationships. It only takes one person to destroy their future.
5. Allow and encourage relationships that enhance their focus on their life purpose.
6. If it doesn't feed, fuel, or fertilize positive focus, forget it.[3]

---

this in chapter 8, but for now, take a look at the competition for your teen's attention.

## SOURCES OF INFLUENCE

If you own a computer or a television, you know that our culture is on information overload. Recent studies indicate that young people today live media-saturated lives, spending an average of nearly six and a half hours a day with media.[4] And, according to recent data, teens spend some of those six-plus hours with more than one medium (for example, listening to music while using the Internet). Consequently, our kids are seeing more and more rapid-fire media images and making countless quick decisions.

This exponential increase in media exposure comes with a historic drop in time spent with adults who provide them with wisdom and direction to navigate life. Studies indicate that since 1960, parents have decreased the time spent with their kids by eleven hours per week. That's ninety minutes fewer per day. The average mother spends less than thirty minutes per day talking with her teens. The average father spends barely eight minutes per weekday in one-on-one conversation with his kids. Fewer and fewer families are eating dinner together. Only 61 percent of our nation's fifteen- and sixteen-year-olds regularly eat dinner with their parents.[5] The increase in uncontrolled and unhealthy information flooding our children's eyes and ears, combined with reduced parental influence, makes it even more difficult for our children to keep focused on what is constructive and foundational to their purpose in life.

## Television

The average teenager spends nearly four hours a day watching television, and thousands of studies consistently indicate the negative impact it has on their behavior. By the time children graduate from high school, they will have watched nineteen thousand hours of television, including two hundred thousand sex acts and about one million acts of violence. Since 1982, television violence has increased by 780 percent, and during that time teachers have observed a nearly 800 percent increase in violence on the school playground.[6] When we think of school violence, Littleton, Jonesboro, Paducah, and other towns come to mind. What were those boys watching on TV while they were young? *She-Ra* and *G.I. Joe* were popular, and these programs displayed about twenty-five acts of violence per hour.[7] Young children in today's emerging generation are watching *Pokémon* and *Power Rangers,* shows that boast about two hundred acts of violence per hour.[8]

In September 2004 *Pediatrics* magazine reported the effect television also had on young people's decisions about sexual intercourse. "The results showed that heavy exposure to sexual content on television related strongly to teens' initiation of intercourse or their progression to more advanced sexual activities (such as 'making out' or oral sex) apart from intercourse in the following year. Youths who viewed the greatest amounts of sexual content were two times more likely than those who viewed the smallest amount to initiate sexual intercourse during the following year or to progress to more advanced levels of other sexual activity. In effect, youths who watched the most sexual content 'acted older': a twelve-year-old at the highest levels of exposure behaved like a fourteen- or fifteen-year-old at the lowest levels."[9]

In 1992 I spoke in schools across the UK. I was overwhelmed with the questions I received about what it was like to be a teenager in America. There was one question I was asked in almost every school I entered: "Are American teenagers just like the ones we see on *90210*?" I talked to thousands of kids who thought everything they saw on television accurately depicted life as an American teenager.

We parents need to remember that television programs and movies are not written or produced *by* kids, but *for* kids, and they do not necessarily represent the views of our children or teens. The scenes we watch on television are written by thirty-somethings, produced by fifty-somethings, and financed by the portfolios of seventy-somethings. When our kids watch a movie like *American Wedding* and see a teenager having sex with a grandmother in a broom closet, they are watching what a team of adults is producing to make money. Therefore, when teens watch one of the top videos of 2003, Fountains of Wayne's "Stacy's Mom," they see a preteen lusting over his girlfriend's mom. At the end of the video, his girlfriend discovers him in the bathroom watching her mother undressing (and fantasizing about her doing a pole dance and undressing for him) while he masturbates. Of course, the girlfriend thinks it's funny. Did I mention that this was one of the most watched teen videos of 2003?

In January 2005 Nielsen released the name of the top television show watched by our nine- to twelve-year-old daughters. Knowing our battle for the focus and dreams of our impressionable girls, I probably shouldn't have been so shocked to read that their favorite television show was ABC's *Desperate Housewives*.[10] My older son is almost nine. I can't help but wonder what his future wife is doing at nine o'clock on Sunday nights. Is she learning what to do if she feels unhappy as a wife? Is the little recorder in her mind watching pornographic scenes of masochistic bondage sex? Will she view marital unfaithfulness as an option for pretty women? I hope not.

## Music

Aristotle said, "Music has a power of forming the character, and should therefore be introduced into the education of the young." Music is the soundtrack of our kids' lives. They are filling almost two hours a day listening to music, and the music they choose is the creed they live by. They listen to twelve thousand hours of music of their own choosing between seventh and twelfth grades, so the messages selected are important ones. Music today isn't Elvis shaking his pelvis. Top 40 music includes themes of violent sex, abuse of women, sex with relatives, oral sex, drug use, murder, and suicide. Many of these songs actually have more explicit downloadable versions on the Internet. There *is* some positive music out there, and many of our kids are choosing it. Aristotle was right. Music can shape character, for good or bad, and it does so every day.

Besides shaping character, the music your son or daughter chooses can tell you volumes about the peers they are trying to associate with and the identity they want to assume. Know, too, that this generation is passionate about its music. When I travel around the country and conduct school assemblies, I talk about specific music artists, and occasionally Insane Clown Posse (ICP) comes up. Most of the teenagers you know probably don't listen to ICP, but the ones who do are among the most troubled I have ever worked with. Passionate and devoted, they view other ICP fans (called Juggalos or Juggalettes) as their family. The e-mail below is from a teenage ICP fan. Although it is heavily edited, you can still hear the passion in his words:

> Listen here *****, The Insane Clown Posse is da...bomb and
> I love them to death and for you guys to say bad ***** bout
> them is like sayin bad ***** bout me and when people do that,
> they get their ***** neck chopped...!!!! And if I was still in
> school I would beg you to come to my school so I could run
> up to you and chop you into little pieces with my machete.

The violence in this e-mail is nothing compared to the lyrics of ICP's music. Do you feel his passion? He is extremely committed to three guys who paint their faces and don't even know his name. But does this teen's choice of music make him violent? Or did he choose it because it crystallizes the emotions he is already dealing with? Either way, don't underestimate the power of music to capture the attention of your son or daughter. And don't be afraid either. I have devoted a large portion of this book to equipping you with ways of dealing with music and other threats, so keep reading.

### The Internet

Nearly all kids have used a computer. In fact, kids today spend about an hour a day online. They visit chat rooms, design personal Web pages, and spend hours instant messaging. And the Internet brings a massive amount of information right to your child's eyes and ears, information that can encourage their healthy focus or distract them from it.

Before the Internet, the average first exposure to pornography was age eleven. Today, five-year-olds are seeing porn. Therapists across the country are treating Internet porn addicts as young as age eight. (The porn industry knows it has to reach your kids young if they want a customer for life.) It's shocking to think that eight out of ten fifteen- to seventeen-year-old kids have had multiple exposures to hard-core pornography, most of them from the Internet.[11]

How many parents would invite a strange man wearing a trench coat into their home to play with their child? Well, that's exactly what we do when we allow our kids to use the Internet without careful supervision.

### Video Games

Nearly three out of four school-aged kids have a video-game system, which they play for about forty-nine minutes per day.[12] And let me tell you, games today are not at all like *PONG*.

*Grand Theft Auto* recently passed *Super Mario Brothers* as the most popular video game of all time. *Grand Theft Auto* involves much more than stealing cars and driving around. The games in this series—*GTA 3, Vice City, San Andreas*—simulate criminal life. Players start as low-level criminals and progress to kingpin status. Along the way they have sex with, beat up, and kill prostitutes, and they kill other people with a variety of weapons, including a golf club, a knife, a chain saw, a gun, and fire. *Grand Theft Auto San Andreas* even allows players to advertise their destructive deeds through tattoos in the exact same way real gangs use tattoos to communicate their criminal accomplishments.

The impact these games are having on our kids is still being researched. We do know, though, that video games have been used since the Vietnam War era to train our soldiers and that school shooters often do exactly as they have trained on their home simulators. In Jonesboro, Arkansas, for example, two middle-school students pulled a fire alarm, set up a military kill zone, and opened fire on students and faculty. The military strategy they used was from a video game they loved to play called *Soldier of Fortune.*

Michael Carneal opened fire on a prayer meeting at his Paducah, Kentucky, high school. Witnesses reported that he never moved his feet or fired to the left, right, up, or down. He fired at whatever entered his "screen." And how did he do? Considering that the average trained police officer seven yards away from a target hits it once out of five shots, Carneal's accuracy was nearly at expert level. Out of the ten shots he fired in thirteen seconds, he hit eight people, with one of the misses singeing a girl's hair. That's incredible considering he had never before fired a real gun.

How can we justify marketing such video games both to our military for training in combat and to our kids for entertainment?

### *Peer Community*

As we discussed in chapter 1, Millennials are community driven and motivated by relationships. A great portion of this book is designed specifically to help you use this unique attribute to your advantage. For now, understand the power relationships have in the life of your child or teen.

"Got Weed?" That's what his hat said. He was a slightly over-weight young male walking through a high-school parking lot. At first glance an adult might think, *Boy, that guy sure is rebelling against the system.* But you need to know that rarely are first glances correct with this young generation. I stopped to talk with this teen. As I approached him, I recognized several signs that he was under the influence of marijuana. A quick check through his pockets deter-mined that he did, in fact, have weed. Why would a guy who had an illegal substance in his pocket put a sign on his body that would alert adults to his use and possession? Isn't he afraid of getting caught?

If you or I had a drug problem, we'd hide it so we could keep our

Seventeen ounces of Southern Comfort is all it takes for me to make new friends. It is all I had to offer to the goddesses of my idolatry: the student council president, the captains of the girls' softball team, the girls voted "most daring" and "most talkative" in the junior-high yearbook. I give it up gladly.

I'd like to think I want to share because it means I have to drink less, but the truth is I like the attention. Now that they know I drink, girls invite me to their houses; they reach for Happy Birthday napkins to write down their phone numbers. In a matter of minutes, everyone has gathered around me like I am the one about to blow out the birthday candles.[13]

—KOREN ZAILCKAS, describing her initial descent into her battle with alcohol jobs and stay out of jail. But that's not the way this generation thinks. Their choices are based on their values. For them (like us), all behavior has a consequence; everything we do can give us something we want. An action might have negative consequences, so we weigh the benefits and consequences in our minds and make a choice. If the benefit is worth the possible negative consequences, we go for it. If not, we don't.

For the young man in the parking lot, his "Got Weed?" hat was a desperate cry to connect. It should have read, "Please be my friend. I don't fit in anywhere, and I am willing to give you drugs if you will pretend to like me." This teen weighed the consequences and made a choice. The pain of being alone was much greater than the pain of getting caught. Decision made.

Every day children and teenagers send out such messages. They paint the name of their favorite band on their backpacks. They do so not because they really, really like the music, but because the ideals and image surrounding the band is the culture they believe they will be able to connect with and be a part of.


## MAKING CULTURE WORK FOR THEM

The media, teen entertainment, and other voices that are successfully impacting today's youth culture all do one powerful thing: they let the uniqueness of this generation work for them. As I've said, some of today's most successful television shows are real and relational in nature. This generation doesn't necessarily buy into everything they see and hear, but these popular reality programs provide a level of authenticity that is attractive to the Millennials. *American Idol, The Real World, Fear Factor,* and other reality shows definitely have an advantage in the battle for this generation's attention.

Also appealing is relational programming that allows kids to assume the identity of a character they either feel they are most like or who possesses attributes they wish they had. *The Sims, Final Fantasy, Grand Theft Auto,* and other video games allow teens to experiment in nontraditional, criminal, and fantasy lifestyles. These relational games let kids live a false reality with very little risk of real-life consequences.

Many Internet sites provide a similar opportunity. MySpace.com is a network of Web sites built by kids. The pictures some kids post to their personal pages often flaunt drug use, self-mutilation, suicidal poses (guns to the head), and other questionable content. Our sons and daughters can try out an image online that they think will bring them relationships. It's not uncommon for teenagers to have between one hundred and two hundred fifty different MySpace friends linked to their site. For kids who feel like they don't have many authentic relationships, the Internet and companies like MySpace remove geographical limitations to friend selection and allow teens to emphasize attributes they want to promote, which at the same time enables them to hide traits they feel self-conscious about.

## PARENTAL GUIDANCE ~~SUGGESTED~~ REQUIRED

Do the math. All of the hours teens spend watching television, listening to music, and sitting in front of computer and video-game screens don't leave many waking hours for us, the parents, to be with our kids. And the probability that our kids successfully navigate their way through these key years without regrets is much smaller. Our silence leaves teenagers free to embrace entertainment that supports their worldview and ideals. Take a glimpse into the life of this young man and see what I mean:

> I am one of the troubled youths. I grew up in a ***** home, I've played plenty of violent video games, almost every person I've ever truly trusted has broken it to an unforgiving level.... I am the kind of person who has the capability of mowing down a school full of innocent people. I'm an avid Marilyn Manson listener. Unlike 99.9 percent of his fans, I actually understand his lyrics, and so forth.
>
> I've grown up in a home with domestic abuse, I was mentally abused a lot, my mother was an alcoholic who was overprotective of me, my father was an angry two-faced *****, and the people I trusted broke my trust in ways that cannot be repaired.... I think the main motivator of a need to commit violence would be a sense of powerlessness.... See, violence might be a weak man's last resort for power, but at least he gains it.... Violence is the solution to someone being an ***** to you. Understanding, forgiveness, talking, blow that *****. Actions speak louder than words, and if people know that you will get whoever crosses you, whoa, that stops 'em. Sorry, man. Peace doesn't always work, the universe isn't made of love, God isn't looking out for me, nothing is there except myself.

"I am the kind of person who has the capability of mowing down a school full of innocent people." "Violence is the solution to someone being an ***** to you." As disturbing as such statements are, I believe these words would pack less punch if they were written by an injured and abused individual whose worldview is void of hope. With the lack of positive parental input in this young man's life, the influence of his entertainment takes on alarming significance.

Clearly, our teens need our wisdom and our guidance. That's why, in the next chapter, we will discuss one more voice in our teens' world—the voice of the family.

# The Interactive
# Training Center:
# The Family

I f the average parent has only about twenty minutes of meaningful contact with his or her teen each day, that means we parents
are frantically chasing behind the screaming voices in our teens' lives
and having far less impact. But the verdict is in, and we are hands-
down the winner. There is no greater influence in the lives of children than parents. That's good news.

## WITH INFLUENCE COMES RESPONSIBILITY

Remember the weatherman? Sometimes he looks at the triple Doppler
radar, studies the atmospheric conditions, and then, relying on his
experience and training, makes predictions and issues warnings. The

weatherman can't always give us good news, because he can't control the weather. If he is to be accurate, he must be impartial.

Like the weatherman, I too use a radar system. My radar does not rely on any technology. The tools I use have arms and legs and sometimes braces. They wear clothing we often don't care for and metal objects piercing every imaginable part of their bodies. They are American teenagers—our sons and daughters. I use the techniques taught in this book to be a part of their lives and interact with them. Of course, I don't rely only on kids. I also study the atmospheric conditions. I pick the brains of today's most brilliant cultural observers and other experts who study the world of young people. I study trends, voices, and other factors that affect my overall prediction. In this chapter I will share what I have observed and what my radar system has revealed about the atmosphere our kids live in.

Unlike the weatherman, I will not only reveal the conditions but also some ways to handle conditions. I will empower you to make an impact on both the conditions in your home and the direction of your child's life. You can use your position as a parent to strategically limit negative influences and maximize positive influences. First, though, let's take a look at the impact—for better or for worse—that families have on children.

## THE INTERACTIVE TRAINING CENTER

The Interactive Training Center is called the family. Since families are the place designed for our children's growth and development, we shouldn't be too surprised that they actually work. For better or for worse, family dynamics have a tremendous impact on young people. One student immediately comes to mind.

Andre was one of those guys always in the middle of everything. If you've ever worked with students in a school environment, you know exactly the type of student I'm talking about. If drama was brewing, there was Andre. If there was a fight, Andre was always near, cheering them on. Although he himself rarely got into physical confrontations, his name always seemed to come up when fights occurred. Andre was, for lack of a better word, frustrating. As I developed a relationship with Andre, I couldn't figure out why this happy-go-lucky guy was so determined to instigate physical confrontations. One day I caught a rare glimpse into Andre's life, and it helped me understand him.

Andre got into a disagreement with another student. The situation escalated to the point where Andre made plans to meet the other student after school and fight him. Andre clearly didn't want to fight this other boy, and he did something after school that really impressed me. He went home and told his father. Andre walked through the front door of his house and said, "Hey, Dad, you'd be proud of me. This boy at school wants to fight me right now, and I decided not to." I think you would agree that Andre made a decision to take the high road, but unfortunately that's not the end of the story.

Andre's father grabbed a sock and some ball bearings, put the ball bearings inside the sock, and tied a knot in it. "Get in the van!" he ordered Andre. Confused, Andre complied. His dad informed him that they were going to the fight and that nobody was going to intimidate his son. After all, Dad had been a Blood in his earlier gang days.

When they arrived at the shopping center where the fight was to take place, a crowd had already formed. Dad handed his son the homemade weapon and said, "When he turns his head, swing!" They got out of the van and confronted the other boy. After Andre's dad made several threats to his son's adversary, the boy said, "I'm not gonna fight your dad. I'm outta here." Dad signaled for Andre to swing. With one swing of the steel-filled sock, the back of the other boy's head split open.

Andre had not gone home and talked to his father so he would build a weapon for him, train him in its use, and instruct him to maim another boy. Andre had attempted to do the right thing. On that day I understood the battle that had been going on inside Andre for years. I realized that his personality and anger were nothing like his father's, yet his father's life influenced him so strongly that he constantly battled with trying to please and connect with him.

## DELINQUENT BEHAVIOR AND FAMILIES

Researching the family structure of delinquent teenagers is not a new concept. As early as the nineteenth century, officials at New York State's Auburn Penitentiary studied the lives of incarcerated men in an attempt to discern the causes of crime. Results (reported in 1829) suggested that family disintegration due to death, desertion, or divorce of parents led to undisciplined children who eventually became criminals.[1] When you take a look at the families of kids who commit crimes, you find some startling facts. If you go back thirty years, you will find that the rise in violent crimes among teenagers parallels the rise in families abandoned by their fathers. Statistically,

## Tips from the Trenches

*What are some of the parenting challenges along the way that I need to be aware of?*

S. Staples: You are dealing with another person with feelings and hopes and fears just like you. Don't expect them to always react perfectly. The hardest lesson for me is that sometimes *they* were right and *I* was wrong. When that happened, I tried to tell them that honestly and apologize for my own mistakes. Also, peers can be stronger influences than parents. Watch the friends they choose and help them choose wisely.

T. Baehr: The mass media of entertainment is avaricious and ubiquitous.

C. Holland: Their world is much different from yours. Be prepared for the shock that they may not agree with everything you do.

R. Johnson: You can take good kids and give them wrong influences and they can go bad. And sometimes as parents we are in too much of a hurry to find a solution, rather than probing deeper and find what's going on in our child's heart. Don't just treat the symptom; identify the cause.

a 10 percent increase in the percentage of kids living in single-parent homes brings about a 17 percent increase in juvenile crime.[2] Even in our highest crime neighborhoods, we see that 90 percent of kids from safe and stable homes do not engage in criminal activities. In contrast, only 10 percent of kids from unsafe and unstable homes in those same neighborhoods avoid criminal behavior.[3] Apparently teenage criminal behavior often has its roots in the habitual deprivation of parental love and affection going back as far as early infancy. Future criminals invariably have a chaotic and disintegrating family life.[4]

While working as a police officer in a housing development, I responded to a domestic-disturbance-in-progress call. As I arrived at the housing unit, I noticed a man lying on his side next to the front porch. His abdomen had been sliced open to the point that his intestines were literally coming out of his body cavity. I drew my weapon from its holster as I confirmed that medics and my backup were en route. As I entered the townhouse, I announced that I was a law enforcement officer and slowly followed the trail of blood through the house.

As I went around the corner into the kitchen, I saw a hysterical young woman with a bloody butcher knife in her right hand. I glanced to her left and observed a three- or four-year-old boy. He captivated my attention. Though my heart was pounding and adrenaline surged, this boy just stood there, not crying, not trembling, not reacting in any way.

Even after securing the crime scene, I couldn't get the boy's face out of my mind. I could see in his eyes that his little recorder was going. His mental notepad was out, and he was watching the situation that had just occurred. I remember thinking, *That little boy has just had a lesson on how to deal with conflict. In ten years, I will be seeing him again.*

Experts tell us that by the time a child is six years old, habits of aggression and anger are already formed.[5] They also tell us that the relationship between parents, not just parent and child, has a powerful effect on very young children. Kids who watch their parents fight regularly may react by disobeying, crying, hitting other children, and exhibiting other antisocial actions. The Department of Justice lists over twenty-one major studies that clearly show the link between parental conflict and delinquency.[6] Some studies even indicate that a child is automatically considered at high risk of committing a crime if his family breaks up within the first five years of his life.[7] The Wisconsin Department of Health and Social Services (now Health and Family Services) conducted a study in 1994 that looked at the family status of delinquent juveniles in state custody and found that only 13 percent had parents who were currently married and living together. In contrast, 44 percent had parents who were never married; 29 percent, divorced; 6 percent, married and widowed; 4 percent, married and separated; and 4 percent, unknown.[8]

It has been said that people who are abused abuse others. A 1998 study of fourteen juveniles condemned to death in the United States seems to support that idea. It revealed that twelve of the juveniles had been brutally abused and five had been sodomized by relatives.[9] As extreme as these cases may be, there is consistency between a child's family environment and future behavior.

## THE AMERICAN FAMILY

I realize that as you read this you are probably thinking about your child and the choices you have made over the years. But let's take a view from the blimp again, widen the lens, and look at families across the nation.

The band Green Day wrote a song called "Jesus of Suburbia," considered by many to be an anthem for this generation. They colorfully describe family life by singing, "Get my television fix sitting on my crucifix, the living room or my private womb. While the *moms and Brads* are away" (emphasis added). Clearly, traditional mom-and-dad homes like in *Leave It to Beaver* seem fictitious to many growing up in a generation who know more about "Mom and Brad" than Mom and Dad. At the turn of the millennium, 69 percent of American kids lived with two parents, down from 77 percent in 1980. Almost one in five children lived with only their mother, and about one out of every twenty-five lived with only their father. When we consider ethnic breakdowns, we see that 77 percent of white, non-Hispanic children lived with two parents, while only 38 percent of African American children and 65 percent of Hispanic children have that situation.[10] Families in the twenty-first century are more complex than the Ozzie and Harriet scenario of the fifties. It is unrealistic to assume that every family today will resemble the idealistic classic television model of what a family should look like. In 2000, the number of single moms raising children grew to ten million from three million in 1970, and single-dad households grew from 393,000 to two million.[11] Married-couple households dropped from 55.2 percent of all households in 1990 to 51.7 percent in 2000,[12] and the number of homes with married couples who live with their own kids fell from 26.3 percent of all homes in 1990 to 24.1 percent in 2000.[13] Although it is ideal to have a father, mother, and children living happily in the same house, we must each learn to work with the reality we awake to each morning.

Whatever its makeup, every family must maximize its uniqueness to work for the common good of all. After all, a strong sense of family is not automatically attained when a biological mother and father maintain a legal and moral contract. If a father and mother are not working as one to bring their family into its purposes, there will be dysfunction. But when everyone in a family contributes to the mission of the family, the synergy is tremendous. If a single mom, a cousin, and a grandmother live together each day and share the same aspirations and dreams for a family, they too can have success. Every family is an assortment of one-of-a-kind individuals that will not fit into a cookie-cutter mold or find success in the same generic seven-step plan. In each home, core principles, values, and beliefs must be clearly and consistently communicated in ways that are truly authentic for each family member in order to make the most of the family's unique strengths, no matter what circumstances have occurred in the past. As Bishop T. D. Jakes writes, "Start today to act like a gourmet chef. Carefully and with love, mix all your ingredients together. Stir that pot with compassion and understanding, and season the mix with support, encouragement, and respect. Don't neglect it; it might boil over or burn. Instead, tend to the pot with a watchful eye, let it simmer gently, and the flavors will blend, creating a dish fit for a king."[14]

## PARENTAL ROLES

Mothers play a vital role in the lives of kids. Research indicates that if a child's attachment to Mom is hindered during the first few years of life, permanent harm can be done to that child's ability to attach emotionally to others and to trust them. So it's good news that when asked who they spend the most time with, kids consistently answer, "My mom."

Dad, you too play a vital role in the life of your child. There are things that we need to provide for our sons and daughters that they can get only at home. So let's look at four things fathers must provide for their children.

### *Intimacy*

When it comes to our kids, we need to force ourselves to connect on a deeper level than "How was school today?" If the only time we interact with our kids is to yell at them or tell them to do something, we are dropping the ball. Remember this: Rules without relationship lead to rebellion. Rules with relationship lead to respect.

I am reminded of a story about a middle-school girl in an East Coast city. While walking around the mall one day, she ran into a friend from school. Her friend greeted her and said, "I want you to meet my friend." She introduced her classmate to the thirty-something-year-old man who was with her. "We are a family," she said.

"You can join our family too," the man added. He then explained what she needed to do if she wanted to be a part of his "family." First, she had to share blood with him. She literally had to drink some of his blood and give him some of hers to drink. Second, she had to commit any sex act of her choice with him.

After joining his "family," this young girl felt guilty and decided to report the man to her local police. When the police arrested him, they found nearly sixty kids in this pedophile's "family." What would drive a sixth-grade girl to drink blood and have sex with a strange man? Perhaps it was a lack of connection with her own family. And, Dad, you're key to giving your kids that vital sense of connection.

### Discipline

Let me tell you about a boy named Paul. He was what many would consider a difficult teenager. Growing up in a broken home, he felt like neither parent really wanted him. Although he lived with his mother, she was quite vocal about her desire to force his father to take him. Mom had a very successful career that consumed much of her time. In fact, her business took her away from home for days at a time, and Paul was alone in a huge house without supervision. We can only imagine what happened in this home during the days Mom was away. No rules, no boundaries, and no authority. Although teens might consider such conditions to be utopia, Paul was miserable. Consistent discipline provides structure that is necessary for healthy development. (We'll talk more about this principle toward the end of chapter 8.)

### Love

It's no secret that our kids need to know we care about them. Telling them that we love them is good, but communicating the message with our actions is even better. When I was a young baseball player, I wanted to pitch. With my dad's encouragement, I asked my coach if I could try pitching. The coach answered, "You can't pitch. You ain't got no arm." I was disappointed. Several weeks later my dad and I went to the sporting-goods store, where he purchased a catcher's mitt, a new baseball, and a home plate. My dad informed me that he had permission to use the school gym every Tuesday and Thursday night and that he would teach me to pitch. Two days a week my father took me up to the school and let me pitch to him. I knew he had other things he wanted and needed to do, but he made sure to be there with me week after week.

## Tips from the Trenches

*What advice would you give someone beginning to parent a teenager?*

S. Staples: First, expect some opposition. Even reasonable limits will be tested. Second, listen even when you know you are right. Teenagers need to know that their ideas have value and merit even if we disagree. Third, be patient. They won't think you're an idiot forever—just until they are twenty-one or so!

C. Holland: Love them and try to understand them and their world. Don't try to make them like you; let them have their own personality within the confines of your moral ethics. Make them a more important part of your life. It's tough for them out there in the world.

The next year I pitched my first no-hitter in a tournament game against the same coach who had said I didn't have an arm. I got the game ball, and my dad wrote on it in marker, "He ain't got no arm." And to this day I have our home plate in my office. It symbolizes an act of extravagant love. It also reminds me that there are no shortcuts to making my boys know they are special to me.

Parents occasionally ask, "Danny, how do I tell my daughter I love her? I don't know what to do." Dads, remember when you were dating your wife? Remember how anemic the words "I love you" felt compared to what was in your heart? If you were anything like me, you would look for all kinds of ways to communicate your love for

> S. Johnson: Hold your kids accountable. Know where your kids are going. Don't be afraid to make a call to make sure they are where they said they were going to be. Don't quit parenting just because they look like they are nearly grown. Don't lose your courage as a parent because they start to talk and act like they are adults. You have to have the same intensity in parenting now that you had when they might run into traffic. You still have to be engaged. In fact, in many ways you have to be more engaged. Just because they have lived eighteen years doesn't qualify them for adulthood. We still keep tabs on them.
>
> B. Waliszewski: Buy a ski boat!

her, and you knew what to do because she captivated you and you studied her. We need to study our kids and look for opportunities to demonstrate our love for them. Handing over a credit card to make up for not spending time with them might bring some excitement, but no material items can fill the void within them that is designed for their parents' love.

## Value

We communicate our values by our actions, so it is vital that we treat our teenagers as the special individuals they are. They need us to be their biggest fans and to encourage them in the things they enjoy doing. Here are some questions to consider:

*Where do you spend your time?* As I already noted, sociologists tell us that more than one-third of the current work force is opting for nontraditional jobs. In other words, many of today's parents are making choices to spend more time with their families. But what about those of us who don't have that option? The right combination of quality and quantity of time can be instrumental. Teach your kids to golf; plan a shopping trip; attend all of their sporting events or concerts. These are simple ways to show you value them.

*When you are spending time with your kids, where is your mind?* While half of all parents (56 percent of dads and 44 percent of moms) *think* their child would like them to spend more time together, only 15 percent of kids say they want more dad time and just 10 percent want more mom time. On the other hand, kids say they want Mom and Dad to be less stressed (30 percent) and to make more money (23 percent). Apparently, kids see lack of money as a cause of stress and a reason why, when we are with them, our minds are somewhere else. Our kids want more quality time *in addition to* more quantity of time.[15]

My family and I frequently visit a small Italian restaurant for pizza. From time to time a father will come in with his teenage son. They always sit in the same booth facing each other. Dad will sit down, open the paper, and leave the son sitting there, reading the back of the paper. How do you think that boy feels about how much his father values him?

Dad, when you are in a meaningful conversation with your child and your cell phone rings, what do you do? Do you interrupt your time together and pick up that phone? One of my mentors, Ron Johnson, told me that he has learned to turn off his cell phone when he is with any of his four sons. What a simple and powerful way to communicate that you value your children.

*Where are you spending your money?* I have friends who sincerely love their kids, yet they fill their lives with hobbies that take them away from their kids during the little time they could have together. From personal watercraft to exotic motorcycles, these forms of entertainment are not bad in and of themselves. But are we dads using our resources to create opportunities to be with our kids or to entertain ourselves without them? Sure, it is healthy to maintain a strong relationship with your wife and spend time with her away from the kids. But do you habitually find your pleasure with your children or away from them? What is ideal is finding an activity that is fun for all.

My wife and I decided one day to make an investment in our boys. We needed another form of transportation, so we went to the Jeep dealership and bought a white Wrangler Rubicon. It was so much fun to drive around with the top down and the two boys bundled up in the back. Every little trip to the store, McDonald's, or the bank became a memorable experience—not to mention the trips we took to the beach. When we're considering anything from vehicles to hobbies, we make decisions to invest time in our sons so they will see how much we value them.

Intimacy, discipline, love, value—these four needs are essential for parents, especially fathers, to fill. Now I realize that, statistically, many who read this book are single parents. All hope is not lost if you are a single mom or dad. Being aware of these four needs will help you use your time with your teenagers intentionally and strategically. Single mothers can do the best they can to be mothers and then get extended family members or other men involved in the lives of their children. Involving extended family will help you avoid burnout and allow you to select the best influences for your son or daughter.

## WHEN NEEDS AREN'T FILLED

If you examine some of the reasons teenagers make destructive decisions and get involved in dangerous activities, you will probably find that one or more of the needs we just discussed (intimacy, discipline, love, value) is not being met at home. To fill the void, some teenagers turn to imitations.

### Gangs

It's not difficult to see the appeal of a gang for some kids. A relationally driven individual who is damaged or removed from the family structure that should be meeting his needs will try to meet those needs in whatever way he can. You may or may not know that in order to join most gangs, boys must be "beat in." They have to go through a season where they are physically beaten to earn the right to bear the gang's name, colors, or jersey. They pay a heavy price. Girls are either "beat in" or "sexed in," meaning they have repeated intercourse with several guys from the gang until the guys feel the girls have had enough. From this experience, teenagers get a sense of intimacy, achieving a level of relationship above the average person. They belong.

In addition to providing a sense of intimacy, gangs have strict rules of discipline. There are colors, tattoos, and hand signals that must be displayed at certain times. When greeting others or when a picture is taken, gang members must represent their gang identity according to gang rules or they could be severely beaten. Some gangs, like MS13, actually conduct their meetings near bodies of water in case they have to "discipline" a member. Sometimes the discipline goes too far and results in that person's death.

Gangs also provide a false sense of love. I know several gang members and regularly talk with them. One good thing I have to say about them is that they have an above average measure of loyalty. But the love is not unconditional. It comes at a great price. And it should disturb you and me that there are young girls in our communities who feel that being raped by guys who have no respect for them will meet their needs for love.

Finally, teenagers feel valuable in gangs. They have certain duties and assignments. The higher up the ladder they go, the more valuable they become. The more drugs they move, for instance, the higher they are promoted. If they kill a rival gang member who has been "green lighted," they can get certain tattoos so everyone will know they have killed. If they kill a police officer, they earn even more status and even more value—however illegitimate it is.

Clearly, gangs are imitation families in which a teen's basic needs are met in a warped way. These individuals demonstrate extreme loyalty and, like other young people, possess gifts and abilities to do something spectacular with their lives. But their search to have their needs met has led them into a world that will leave them empty, if not locked up in jail.

## Sex

Many girls crave intimacy and acceptance. When they leave the family to find it, it usually comes in the form of sex. It deeply saddens me when I meet a young girl who has traded her body for attention that looks like intimacy, love, and value. Today's teen entertainment makes this process appear very normal. The most popular genres of teen music—hip-hop and gangsta rap—objectify women with crude references that are often pornographic. Very soon after engaging in this type of relationship, teen girls often discover that they were never loved, and they feel even less valuable than before the act. This causes many young girls to look for other partners, and the imitation cycle repeats itself. Before long they begin to believe the lies about their value, about intimacy, and about what real love looks like.

## WHO WANTS A FAMILY?

Are you ready for some really good news? Nobody in your house wants a family more than your child or teenager does. More than

Mom, more than Dad, more than anyone, your teenager wants a real family.

When asked what influences them the most, more teenagers answer, "My home" rather than school, friends, religion, music, books, television, movies, or magazines. When asked who they look up to the most, they don't answer Eminem, Britney Spears, or any other superstar or athlete. Seventy-nine percent of them say, "My parents." Mom and Dad, you *do* have the greatest influence on your kids.[16]

The Council of Economic Advisers did a study called "Teens and Their Families in the 21st Century" (2000). Their study made an amazing statement about the influence the family can have on decisions kids make. "Over 50 percent of teens who do not have dinner with their parents have sex by age 15 or 16. By contrast, only 32 percent of teens who do eat dinner with parents have ever had sex.... Teens aged 15 to 16 who don't eat dinner with their parents regularly are twice as likely to have attempted suicide." From my own study of families that have successfully raised teenagers, I have learned that something as simple as having meals together often made a huge difference over time, even when parents didn't do everything else right.

## How Does the Interactive Training Center Work?

Many of us are aware of the impact we have on our children, and most of us are intentional about certain things we do as we attempt to shape our kids. For example, we try to be consistent in discipline, to limit their time in front of the television, and to encourage reading and other productive activities. These efforts are all good. But we need to realize that the Interactive Training Center is always working, intentionally or not. Whether you consider your family functional or dysfunctional, it has an influence on your kids. Let's talk about how we can maximize the positive impact of this concept and minimize its negative effects.

## TEACHING VERSUS TRAINING

There is a key element that is impacting and shaping kids. Knowing that it exists will give you, the parent, a greater advantage in reaching your teens. Most of us have sat our kids down and given them talks. We *teach* our kids from our well of knowledge and try to impart vital information. Teaching is an effective way of giving kids information. Let's look at a typical teaching moment.

We sit Johnny down and envision turning on his internal recorder. We then go on to explain why homework is vital to getting good grades, why good grades are vital to getting a good job, and why a good job is vital to success in life. No matter what the topic of our talk, we reach the point where we feel either that we have exhausted the topic or Johnny has grasped the information. At this point we often assume that Johnny has turned off his internal recorder since our talk is over. But teaching isn't the only vehicle we have for getting information to our kids.

Every waking moment our kids are with us, their learning recorders are on. They watch us eat, talk, argue, manage our time, manage our resources, and so on. Every day they watch us live, and by watching us, they are being *trained*. We *teach* kids by sharing what we know, but we *train* them by who we are. I remember the first time I noticed this process in action.

When my son was about two years old, we had a yellow Lab named Bud. He was the most compliant dog on earth, but because Bud was a big dog and we had little kids in the house, we still had to be very strict with him. One day my son decided to discipline the dog. "Bud, NO!" he yelled. I looked over at Bud. He was standing in the corner looking around, rather dumbfounded. It took me a second to realize that my son had never been taught how to discipline a dog, but he had been trained to do it by watching me.

The story of Evan Ramsey, a school shooter from Alaska, also comes to mind. Evan was interviewed by MSNBC about his actions at his Bethel, Alaska, school. Something in that interview jumped out at me. Evan's father, Don Ramsey, had been arrested years earlier for storming the *Anchorage Times* when the paper didn't publish an article he had written. Armed with a small arsenal of weapons, he had fired warning shots into the ceiling and taken people hostage. He later surrendered. Therefore, when dealing with some difficult issues at school, Evan did exactly what his father had trained him to do by his actions. Evan took the same type of weapon, stormed the school, and fired warning shots into the ceiling. Evan was actually assigned to the same jail cell that his father had occupied after his rampage. I seriously doubt Evan's father intentionally taught him how to go on a rampage, but clearly Evan had been trained.

Let me give you another example. Growing up, baby Juan occasionally sees Dad come home from work on Friday in a bad mood. Dad sits in his chair, drinks a few beers, and seems to feel much better. Fourteen years later Juan gets his report card at school and realizes that his social life is pretty much over as he has known it. So Juan goes home and smokes some marijuana. Mom walks in on him and is horrified by his drug use. In this scenario, what did Dad do? He used a *legal* chemical to change the way he felt. What did Juan do? He used an *illegal* chemical to change the way he felt. Juan had been trained.

Very few of us would be pleased to have our vulnerable fourteen-year-olds experimenting with alcohol. In her book, *Smashed: Story of a Drunken Girlhood,* Koren Zailckas describes watching her parents use alcohol at a party once: "There is something in that wine that lights them up from the inside like fireflies settling around us at dusk.... They always seem so much happier then, less alone. And I wish I could preserve that feeling for them, capture them, too, in a mason jar and bring them home aglow."[17] This statement captures the polarized images that young teenagers have to balance when we talk about the negative effects of alcohol but they see firsthand an attractive aspect of its use. The screaming voice of a teen's insecurities seems no match for the pleasant effects of alcohol use.

And we've all dealt with teenage insecurities. Think back to where you were in 1972. If you have teenagers, chances are you were in middle school or high school. Teenagers in 1972 set a record: more of them used marijuana than any other generation in U.S. history, and apparently, that generation is continuing this activity of their youth. Research indicates that 21 percent of them, now middle-aged, are still smoking marijuana. In fact, as drug use declines among teenagers, statistics reveal that more parents of teens are using drugs than the teenagers.[18]

A student I worked with was found at school with a bag of marijuana. A scale, some baggies, and more marijuana were found his car. His mom asked me to talk with him. I sat down with him and said, "Kevin, I don't understand this. You are a brilliant student. Sometimes you have great days, sometimes you don't. What's going on?"

He said, "Danny, when my mom has weed and my dad has coke, everything is fine. If one of them can't get their stuff, it's like living in hell."

I wish I could tell you that was my only conversation with a student who admitted to me that his or her parents also use drugs. How can parents discipline their child when they are doing the very thing they're forbidding?

## THE PARADIGM SHIFT

The power of family lies in how we shape our kids with and without words. Teaching and training are two potent tools for transferring our legacy and imparting our values to our kids. When our training is consistent with our teaching, we gain a synergistic advantage over other influences in our kids' lives. We can communicate values to kids who "don't want to hear it" by living out those values in front of them. We can use teachable moments to teach and train them by living it 24/7. We need to embrace the gift of influence we have been given and deliberately use it to reach our kids.

# Part II

# Meeting the Needs
# of Teens

I was at your assembly today, and I would like to thank you. You've given me hope with myself. Last year I almost killed myself. I'm a writer at heart, and many of my stories are about teens in crisis and the one person who changes their whole life around. I'm choosing one to finish, then I'm going to publish it.

—TEENAGE STUDENT, e-mail correspondence

# Tactical Parenting

I t's been said that the best defense is a strong offense, and there's no better picture of that concept than a sports team. In sports, no matter how good your defense is, you can count on a worthy opponent scoring against you. So if you want to be victorious, you need to score more points than your opponent. Most teams who fail to do this actually crumble from within.

## THE PURPOSE OF PARENTING: STRONG OFFENSE VERSUS STRONG DEFENSE

John Wooden is the legendary former head coach of the UCLA Bruins men's championship basketball team. Now in his nineties, he is still considered by many to be the greatest college basketball coach of all time. With ten NCAA championships (seven consecutive wins) and four undefeated seasons, he certainly is in a class by himself. Whether or not we are basketball fans, we can learn several things about successful coaching from Coach Wooden. In his book *Wooden on Leadership*, Coach Wooden said, "At some point, later than I'd care to admit, it became clear to me that the most productive model for good leadership is a good parent. A coach, teacher, and leader, in my view, are all basic variations of being a parent. And while parenting is the most important job in the world, leadership isn't far behind. I revere the opportunity and obligation it confers, namely, the power to change lives and make a difference. For me, leadership is a sacred trust."[1] Coach Wooden understands the power of coaching our teenagers so they will learn to keep their composure and be able to develop a powerful offensive strategy for life.

From my own experience working with kids, I can tell you that some of the principles active in Coach Wooden's Bruins and other winning teams are also at work in winning families. One of those keys is having a strong offense. When parents encourage their kids to perfect their gifts and pursue their purpose, a very effective offense takes the field. Although their team may get scored on and from time to time decisions may be made that are not productive, that offense will eventually come through for the win.

## ESCAPE THE TUNNEL VISION

When police officers go through a law enforcement academy, much training time is spent learning to handle their firearms. They study shootings and learn the latest techniques for surviving a life-and-death battle. One natural tendency they need to unlearn, though, is tunnel vision. When we're faced with a threat, we automatically direct all available attention and energy to neutralizing that threat. For police officers this presents a serious problem because they must often engage multiple threats simultaneously.

Police officers are trained to fire at their targets and then sweep their eyes to the left and the right before re-holstering their weapons. Why? Because in the past officers were re-holstering their weapons before making sure the scene was clear of other threats. Officers who survived the initial threat but still focused on it even after it was gone were being killed by other threats they never saw. Their tunnel vision kept them from seeing other dangers.

We as parents can fall prey to tunnel vision too. Focused on social influences, peer pressure, and other threats to the moral upbringing of our kids, we wield our parental defensive weapons with tactical excellence. But if we're not careful, we can become so consumed with protecting our sons and daughters that we may ignore the powerful offensive role we also must play as a successful life coach. A dominant, defensive survival mind-set tends to *react* to negative circumstances, influences, and events. Parenting from this posture can limit our role as parents to be emergency responders who engage the dangers to our children's future.

When it comes to our kids, no matter what their age, we need to be strategic and intentional rather than just reacting to negative circumstances. I know many kids who create negative situations to foster interaction with their parents. We parents need to find a balance between being *proactive* and *reactive*. Ask yourself, *Why am I protecting my son/daughter?* When it comes to convincing our teenagers to avoid behavior that could hurt them or cause them painful regrets, a positive reason can be much more compelling than a negative one.

When I turned fifteen, I participated in an abstinence program called True Love Waits. I signed my name on a card pledging that I would not have sex until I was married, and I received a ring from my parents as a reminder of this decision. I have to admit, though, that I thought I would be married by the time I turned eighteen! Twenty-one, twenty-two, twenty-three, twenty-four—the years slowly crept by. What had I been thinking? I began to recall my motivation, envisioning my wedding night, handing the ring to my wife, and seeing the look on her face. I knew she would be able to trust me the rest of our lives because I had been faithful to her before I ever knew her. I knew I would have no regrets, no diseases, no children by other women, and no unwanted faces in my mind. At twenty-five I finally walked down the aisle with my wife. In our hotel room on our wedding night, I handed Amanda my ring and said, "Amanda, before I ever knew you, I loved you enough to save myself for you." My dream of what I wanted my marriage to be like kept me pure. Sure, regrets crossed my mind, but the positive vision of my future compelled me to stay on track.

We parents need to intentionally prepare our children and teenagers for their future by both providing a hedge of protection around them in the form of rules, accountability, and structure, and giving them powerful reasons for doing the right thing. After all, if a coach prepared his team only to stop the opponent's strong offense, his team would still be defeated. As we coach our children, let's not forget our offensive strategy.

## PUTTING OUT FIRES

I truly believe that every person on earth has a specific purpose for being alive. Our kids have a task to accomplish with their lives beyond living well. It is our mandate as parents to help them discover their purpose, prepare them for it, and launch them toward it. When I ask third graders about the dreams they have for their lives, I never hear, "I want to be a crackhead when I grow up." Yet every time I talk to someone whose life is being snuffed out by the consuming addiction to a chemical, I can't help but wonder how she ended up robbed of her dream and having her life waste away.

I had been reaching out to a troubled teenager named Brian. He'd walk down the hallway at school looking like an official poster child for marijuana. Yet something was different about Brian. He was a bright young man who had a keen sense of purpose. One day he walked into my office and shut the door. Arrogantly he said to me, "Do you know I bring three pounds of marijuana to this school every week?"

I sat back in my chair and reflected on his claim. I decided he was testing our relationship by revealing something he knew I hated; he wanted to see if it was safe enough to go deeper. His statement demanded a response. "Brian, let me ask you a question. When you were in third grade, did you raise your hand in class on career day and say that you wanted to be a drug dealer?" The room was silent. Tears filled his eyes as he said, "No. My dad was a great athlete, and I wanted to be just like him. But he got mixed up in drugs, and my mom left him." He went on to describe his rocky family life and adjustment to his mom's new husband. I could almost tell you the exact date that Brian gave up on his dream and began abusing chemicals.

Young people today seem to have a mind-set that all roads lead to happy places, so they appear to roam aimlessly in pursuit of pleasure. In fact, the way some teenagers live, they seem to think they can pull out of their driveway at home, make random left and right turns, and automatically end up at Disney World. Parents, we know that's not the case. That's why we need to help our kids pursue their dreams, to take positive steps that will lead them to the place they want to end up.

## THE JOURNEY TO IDEAL

It is our role as parents to create a backdrop that will enable our kids to safely explore and fulfill their purpose. While attending Regent University, I was exposed to a powerful concept presented by futurist Jay Gary. Although his material was focused more globally than individually, I recognized some very powerful concepts that affect parents today. Since we cannot accurately determine the future, we need to equip our emerging adults with what they will need to survive three possible outcomes on their journey to ideal.

*Probable.* There are stages of life in which the outcome is predictable to a certain degree. As parents or professionals working with teenagers, we have seen the usual results of certain actions. Even though our teenagers may struggle in certain areas, we can predict how their common struggles will probably end.

*Potential.* The roadway to ideal is often filled with hidden variables we'll call *potential*. On the trip our teens might encounter valleys of financial difficulty, marital struggle, disappointment, and failure. How well our kids are prepared to deal with these hidden variables may very well determine whether they end up at their ideal destinations or somewhere else. We equip our kids to deal with potential outcomes by modeling and teaching them proper attitudes, personal responsibility, faith, and techniques for rebounding.

*Preferable.* Most of us hope our teenagers will experience successes and learn from or avoid our mistakes. We would like to see them avoid *possible* hidden variables and rise above *probable* to experience what is *preferable*. If you have more than one teenager, you may have a feeling that one is more likely to experience what is preferable because of her more obvious gifts and compliance to your correction and advice. You may also have one who seems to regularly avoid hazards at the last possible second. I like to call what is preferable "the high road." The fact is, some teenagers will only visit the preferable roadway from time to time and spend more time navigating probable and possible on their way to ideal.

No matter what roadway our kids choose to take or are forced by circumstances to tread, their future will shape them. It is vital for us to help our teenagers prepare for these scenarios while not squelching the gifts and purposes they possess. For those of us who are battle scarred and have tasted our share of disappointment, we could easily destroy the hope of ideal through the lens of what we consider reality. Preparing our teenagers for the future involves more than just helping them avoid difficulty. Preparing them to traverse the terrain of probable, possible, and preferable means equipping them with a balance of reality, hope, and faith.

I believe that ideal isn't a destination; it's a process of preparation that makes us the men and women we were intricately designed by our Creator to be. Ideal is a process that can either shape us to be something great or defeat us. To help our kids avoid defeat, we need to create a backdrop of perseverance for our kids.

Consider the analogy of the chick and the egg. Before a baby chick approaches its entry into full life, it finds itself in a safe and comfortable environment. The chick's home, the egg, feels just perfect. At a certain point, though, the chick has an eye-opening revelation: the same shell that is keeping it comfortable and safe is also restricting its life. So the little chick begins pecking at the shell. The chick may not understand it, but he must continue to peck to grow. As he breaks through the shell, his tenacious hard work enables him to gain the strength and endurance to survive in a new environment. Well-meaning people have tried to help this process by cracking the shell and opening it for the chick. By short-circuiting the process, however, they kill the chick. The chick is unable to handle this new environment for even a few minutes and is stillborn.[2]

The unique nature of each child will dictate how rigorous their journey is to ideal demands, but as parents, we can equip them with the attitude of perseverance necessary to reach their destination. Struggle is not a bad thing if it is producing something positive.


## HINDSIGHT OR FORESIGHT?

As our kids approach the future, we parents have a decision to make about how their transition into adulthood will happen. We can

# TIPS FROM THE TRENCHES

*What are a few things every parent needs to know to see results like yours?*

S. Staples: No results can be guaranteed, but setting reasonable limits with consistent enforcement in a loving way is about as guaranteed as you can get.

C. Holland: That you really love your kids; that they are a priority in your life; that parenting is a lifetime responsibility; that they need you to train them by modeling a lifestyle, not just telling them how to live.

R. Johnson: Consistency, godly character, integrity, maintaining a standard of right and wrong. Kids need to know that they are free to fail and it won't cost them everything. From the time they are young, our kids were given a level of responsibility. Increasing levels of freedom were given to them, and if they blew it, we'd reel them in and give them another chance.

S. Johnson: You can't be selfish and be a successful parent any more than you can be selfish and be a successful spouse.

B. Waliszewski: Don't take shortcuts in your spiritual life. You can't unscramble scrambled eggs, so do it right the first time (the only time). Look for things your children can really excel in and encourage and support—even financially—those things. Remember that the years your children are at home will fly by.

either look behind or look ahead. Those of us who opt for hindsight are pushed into the future while we are still looking backward. From this perspective, we can offer very little positive input about navigating the challenges unique to this generation. However, if we look ahead, we begin to see our children as tools that can be used to impact life as we know it or as they will know it.

Foresight also helps us prevent adverse circumstances. Maybe a path needs to be forged in a direction new to all of us, but we know that our sons and daughters are perfectly equipped for it. Facing the future and knowing the makeup of our teenagers, we are able to point them in directions that are nontraditional and preventive. Parents with foresight are also able to control things that seem uncontrollable. For example, we may feel that we cannot rely on our government to provide financial support for us later in life. But with foresight, we can plan, educate, and model strategies for financial stability that will equip our children to effectively deal with uncertain times. We can also cultivate an atmosphere in our homes of true net worth—that intangible far greater than our material possessions, the one calculated only by valuing the aspects of our lives that money could never buy.

Foresight uses the wisdom of today with the discernment of tomorrow to equip the next generation with the best possible tools for whatever they many encounter. With our eyes on the horizon, no matter how bleak the picture may seem, we can see our teenagers as elements of healing, ingredients of change, and highly customized tools of purpose greater than anything we could comprehend when they were born.

Remember, however, that just because parents have foresight doesn't mean their teenagers will automatically avoid regrets. But when our teenagers make wrong decisions that have long-term consequences, our forward-looking vision is even more vital. Hindsight recalls the past and says, "He'll never learn" or "He'll be locked up just like his father." Foresight says, "You have taken your life down a wrong path, and there are consequences, but this isn't you. This won't be your defining moment."

## THE CRY OF CULTURE VERSUS THE CRY OF PURPOSE

We can see nearly sixteen hundred commercial images each day. All of these ads point out our supposed faults and tell us how their products can improve us.[3] If we have body odor, there is deodorant. If we don't have friends, all we have to do is drink this product and friends will come running. Images all around us scream out that we need certain products and a certain lifestyle in order to rise to *adequacy*. But from deep within each of us, a quiet voice reminds us that we were not created to be adequate but to be *exceptional*. As parents, it is that voice we need to cheer on.

After all, there is a passion that comes from living for something greater than ourselves. As parents, we can either stifle that or enhance it. What's at stake in all this? We really don't know. Remember, it's not our decision but our discovery. I can't help but wonder if the cure for cancer is wrapped up inside a four-foot package with curly hair. Is the next great poet sitting in the back bedroom with his headphones blaring? We don't know, but we have both the power and the duty to help our children discover their future role in this world. Here's how.

## HELP THEM DISCOVER

I believe that my kids, as well as yours, were created for a certain purpose they must discover. Nobody is here by accident. In fact, I believe that each of our kids was created to solve a specific problem. But there is a huge difference between deciding a child's purpose and the child discovering it.

Teenagers are a vital part of our society. Whether your teenager will become a soldier fighting tyrants or a doctor whose steady hand will remove cancerous tumors, his gifting and purpose will benefit others. One day someone in need will cry out for the gift that is inside him, and if he meets that need, he will be the answer to that person's prayer. There is not another person on earth like him. No matter who he is or how he has been labeled, others will suffer if he makes choices that keep him from developing his gifts and fulfilling his purpose. In fact, I believe that each of us has been created with weaknesses so we will come alongside others who have strengths in those areas.

But how do we help our teens discover their gifts and their purposes? Let's first examine their gifts.

### Gifts

All people have specific gifts that make them unique. If we are going to help our kids identify their gifts, we have to put aside our predetermined ideas about what we think they should do with their lives. I've heard parents say, "Your grandfather was a Marine, your father is a Marine, and you will be a Marine." That may be true, but that child's gifts may be very different from the typical disposition that makes a great Marine.

Gifts are like seeds that are planted to produce fruit and more seeds. The gifts inside your teenager can produce something great on this planet. Those gifts may enable her to impact other people's lives far beyond what she is probably imagining. To follow are some basic questions that may help your son or daughter discover their gifts.

*What do they love?* What they really enjoy doing may be a clue to the special skills and gifts they have. Not only is love a clue, but it also has a special ability to equip an individual for her purpose. That's because love goes beyond drawing them toward their purpose; it is the fertile soil that produces specialized knowledge and uncommon wisdom. For example, when a teenager truly loves music, she hears more than a guitar. She can identify the model of the guitar, the type of strings, plus the amp and processor used. Loving something motivates interest in how it works, which then cultivates related learning and abilities.

*The cry of our culture is to rise to adequate. The cry of our purpose is to become exceptional.*

*What do they love to talk about?* You may notice that one of your children will clam up when talking about animals or other children, but when the conversation turns to computers, he or she can't stop talking.

*What subjects do they get excited about?* If money were not a factor, what would they want to do with their lives? There is a huge difference between a job and a vocation. By definition, a vocation is a *call.* A vocation has its sights set outwardly, while a job focuses on making money and attaining other goals. We often encourage our kids to find a job doing something with their gifts that they *can do.* As my good friend Dr. Jeff Myers once said, "A vocation is something you cannot *not* do." As well-meaning parents, we often catch a glimpse of that purpose in our child, but our doubt rises up and we advise them to get some education or experience in something they can "fall back on." We need to wisely encourage them to explore their gifts and not let our fears and doubts snuff out their small flames of hope of becoming exceptional.

*The cry of our culture is to rise to adequate. The cry of our purpose is to become exceptional.* I cannot emphasize enough the importance of this idea. Teenagers are keenly aware of the negatives in their lives. They know what they are not good at, and they are wise to try to overcome the flaws they are capable of changing. We are wise if we encourage our teens to strengthen what is already strong in their lives. It is not peer pressure, media influence, or any other external pressure that causes a teenager to self-destruct. It is the death of a dream. The undiscovered gifts of our children are one of America's greatest tragedies. Therefore, we need to help our kids recognize what makes them unique and help them build their future around it.

## Purpose

While gifts are honed and developed for maximum effectiveness, purpose often beckons vaguely in the distance and only becomes clearer as we walk the journey. Purpose is the calling on our lives. It is much more than a buzzword or a catchy abstract concept. Knowing our purpose is what establishes us. Purpose answers the biggest questions in our lives, including the whys. Many teenagers I meet have more questions than answers. Many of the songs our teens embrace ask riveting questions without providing any answers. Those of us who know our purpose find answers to such questions. People who don't determine their purpose often struggle to establish a life that they feel is really worthy of their time on earth, and they experience extreme emptiness and lack of direction. Purpose infuses substance into every activity of our lives.

Purpose gives dreams the guidance and direction necessary to bring them into reality. Purpose is the *why* behind the *what*. When teenagers have purpose, each decision they make takes on greater value. We parents must do two things if we want our teenagers to understand and operate in their purpose.

## BEING PARENTS OF PURPOSE

First, we need to recognize our own purpose. In other words, we are more likely to raise kids with an intentional purpose-centered life if we live our own lives according to our purpose. But many of us really haven't established the why behind what we do in our own lives. Why do I need a new car? more money? a promotion? a bigger house? a certain image? Is living comfortably my purpose in life? These things are not inherently good or bad. You may require a new vehicle so you can impact more lives. Your house may be a resource your family can use to serve others in your community. You may need that promotion so you can better help your children learn to live out their purposes.

However, when our decisions consistently conflict with our purpose, we live a life that lacks authenticity. Lack of authenticity causes us to live below our potential and for a less significant reason. Let's be honest: we aren't on earth to impress the neighbors or just acquire nice stuff. Our lives are worth much more. As a rule, if something is not worth dying for, it's not worth living for either.

## BEING FAMILIES OF PURPOSE

Besides being parents of purpose, we need to discover, establish, and document our family's purpose. After all, a family is more than just a father, mother, and kids living together.

My father gave me some useful advice when I was considering getting married. He told me to know where I was going in life and marry the woman who was going in the same direction. Okay, he had a few thousand other qualifying statements that went with this, but for the purposes of this book, that's what he said. Although Amanda and I grew up in different families, we were two individuals going in the same direction. We were best friends, and we knew God wanted us to be together.

We started our journey together with a desire to use our gifts, abilities, and time to make an eternal difference in our generation. We were not willing to live our lives for anything that wasn't worth dying for in our eyes. As our family grew, that purpose expanded to include shaping our boys into the unique men of faith, boldness, and character they were created to be.

Being loyal to our family purpose hasn't been natural or easy. Several years into our marriage, we found our lives running exactly as we had planned. We had a very nice house in a very nice neighborhood with one toddler, one infant, and the perfect dog. I was a professional youth worker, and Amanda stayed at home with the kids just as we had planned. But bad news came the day the organization I had worked with for seventeen years informed me that they could no longer pay my salary. Amanda and I did what we had to do to survive. I worked from seven in the morning until three in the afternoon, Monday through Friday, as well as most weeknights, teaching computer classes at a local technical school. Amanda worked weekends. I remember the day we sat down and revisited our purpose. Raising our boys was more important than working all the time in order to have a nice house and fancy cars.

We sold the house and the cars, and we got a much cheaper house and a Plymouth Acclaim with almost two hundred thousand miles on it. Let me tell you, the proverbial Joneses were nowhere in sight. But the purpose of our lives wasn't to keep up with them by living beyond our means and sacrificing our opportunity to model for our boys a purpose-centered life. We have reaped tremendous fruit in our boys' lives because of the choices we made in those rough times, choices that were guided by our family purpose. In contrast, aimless families produce aimless kids.

Once families discover and establish their purpose, it is very important to document it. A family mission statement is a plumb line to measure decisions in our lives. In *The 7 Habits of Highly Effective*

*Families,* Stephen R. Covey writes that a family mission statement "is a combined, unified expression from all family members of what your family is all about—what it is you really want to do and be—and the principles you choose to govern your family life."[4] What a great way to help your teenager develop independence that has a purpose.

Your teen might know his areas of gifting and be on his way to developing them, but he may have only a vague idea of his purpose. To follow are a few questions to help your teen discover his purpose.

*What upsets your teen? What makes her cry? What fills her mind and heart with compassion?* Answering these three questions with some consistency can help your teen determine what her life will *heal.* Whatever your children sincerely care about to the point of tears may be a clue as to what their gifts and purposes will *cure.*

*What makes your teen livid? What injustice or action fires him up?* These answers may very well point to something his gifts will *transform.* We are not all made to fight every battle, but some people have a passionate anger toward a specific injustice or issue that empowers them to address and improve that situation.

*What does your teen do that makes her feel more alive?* Many of our kids walk through life feeling like square pegs in a world full of round holes. We can either choose to embrace that uniqueness or try to force them into molds that don't work for them. When we force our kids into holes they were not designed to fit into, all of their energy will be spent on survival. But when square-peg teenagers enter square-peg roles, they are energized and may rise to a level of excellence beyond what you are used to seeing them attain. This energy and excellence are great indications that they may be doing something they were created to do.

*What is it that your teen cannot* not *do?* My sons are different from each other. Although they came from the same parents, one is, for example, far more introverted than the other. One weekend I was preparing to do some yard work, and my older son asked me if he could help. He loves to take on projects and accomplish tasks, but even more, he is a verbal leader at heart.

"Dad, can I edge the driveway?" Josh asked.

"Sure," I responded as I got the manual edger out of the garage. I began cutting the grass and lost sight of him. When I returned to the garage to get gas, I saw Josh supervising a work crew of neighborhood friends. Some had brooms, some had other tools, but all were working hard at cleaning up after Josh's edging job. Josh hurried over to me and asked, "Dad, can I get some money and pay them?"

There is no question that Josh has a gift of verbal leadership, and he cannot do any task without recruiting others and giving motivation and instructions. He has been designed to do things that way.

My other son, Caleb, is not a motivational peacemaker like his brother. He can best be described as a compassionate warrior. Even when we horseplay around the house, Caleb always rescues the underdog, and he is just a little more serious than the rest of us. He tenaciously rights wrongs and corrects injustices, and he will compassionately bend down to shake a baby's hand without caring what his peers may think. Caleb is also fascinated with the last three days of Christ's life, and he cannot be separated from his *Passion of the Christ* spike necklace. There is no question both of my boys have the makings to be heroes in their generation, yet in very different ways.

*What does your teen feel needs to be done with excellence?* This question might be easier to answer than you think. Is there an area of interest where good just isn't good enough? That hunger for excellence is an indication of a passion for something he feels strongly about. Explore that hunger and you will help him discover something powerful about himself.

*What has your teen accomplished in her life that brought her great satisfaction?* While working in one public school, I looked for a creative way to connect with teenagers that gave them a reason to come into my office and talk without the stigma of having a problem. I decided to dedicate one wall of my office to pictures of students. The only criterion I had for hanging a picture was that it had to be a picture of them doing something they enjoyed. I can still see the pride on one boy's face as he boldly entered my office with his Polaroid picture in hand. Nate lived with his single mother, struggled with depression, and was labeled special ed for his low level of reading. No matter how hard he tried, he always seemed to struggle to find his niche. His countenance as he walked through my doorway that day reminded me of a fairy-tale hero who just rescued a damsel in distress. He gave me a picture of himself riding a rail with in-line skates. His boosted confidence made me think of a sailboat in the middle of a calm lake when a surge of wind hits its sail. I don't know if Nate is a great reader today or not, but I can tell you that he has a great family and a career in public service.

Your teen might enjoy computers, music, skating, or something else completely off the wall. I encourage you to think outside the box. Teens are likely to continue pursuing those areas where they find success.

## HELP THEM PREPARE FOR THE JOURNEY

Once our children have an idea of their gifts and/or purpose, preparation can begin. No matter how young our kids are, we parents can start positioning them to limit distractions and can guide their attention to what will be necessary for a successful journey. This means we focus their time, energy, and creativity. I get very concerned when I see kids filling their lives with activities without purpose. I'm certainly not saying that they shouldn't play sports or do other fun things, but when they need a Day-Timer to keep up with their schedules, maybe we need to take a step back and see how well we are protecting their focus and attention. Begin with the end in mind, as Stephen Covey advises:

> To begin with the end in mind means to start with a clear
> understanding of your destination. It means to know where
> you're going so that you better understand where you are now
> and so the steps you take are always in the right direction.
>
> It's incredibly easy to get caught up in the activity trap, in
> the busy-ness of life, to work harder and harder at climbing
> the ladder of success only to discover it's leaning against the
> wrong wall.[5]

How often do we see four-year college educations for our children turn into seven years with three majors? If our kids don't begin their education with the end in mind, they may not end up where they want to be.

Our kids also need to know that things are created twice. As Covey describes, things are first created in our minds, and then they're created physically. Planning is absolutely essential to accomplishing purpose and dreams. Champions don't become champions in the ring. They're made in the daily routine and preparation time. It's our task to pull the champion out of our sons and daughters. The passion that helped reveal their purpose will also fuel their preparation.

---

*A ship in the harbor is safe, but that's not what ships are for.*
—JOHN A. SHEDD

---

Doug Baggett is a top high-school basketball coach. He has a rare gift to draw individuals far beyond their visible ability. He consistently builds winning teams. One of his secrets is that he doesn't make talent the primary factor when putting together a team. Talent without passion to develop it is wasted. He calls it heart. He would cut a player with talent if the player didn't have the heart to work.

Doug's basketball players develop nicknames for each other that reveal attributes about them. I remember watching practice once and seeing a player they called Tin Man. I asked one of the guys why they called him Tin Man. Referring to *The Wizard of Oz*, he replied, "Because he doesn't play with heart."

Too often I see well-meaning family members carelessly wielding their opinions about their young loved one's future with no regard for the impact their words will have. We need to understand that the words we speak have tremendous power in the lives of young people, especially the ones we are closest to. Some of the most painful memories teens have shared with me have been words spoken by loved ones, often made as observations rather than malicious attacks. We need to be especially careful with our words when our kids lay their most precious and fragile dreams before us. Sometimes our well-intentioned attempts to bring so-called reality into the picture can be more harmful than beneficial. A good friend of mine wrote a book aptly titled *Dream Thieves,* specifically about people like this. If we are not intentionally creating an environment where our teens' dreams can mature, we may be causing damage to their futures.

## FOUR STEPS OF PREPARATION

Our sons and daughters will need to take four steps if they are to effectively move from a vague sense of purpose to a vocation with a powerful impact on their world. As life coaches we can help them work through these four steps, but we cannot prepare for them. Also, these are not the only steps, but they are a good start.

### 1. Examine Past Experiences

Our kids need to take an inventory of their life experiences. Some of those experiences will help them define their purpose. Other experiences may have warped their view of their gifts. Or, if they have gone through trauma or other powerful emotional struggles, they may be living their lives to prove someone wrong, to avoid something negative, or to rebel. Recognizing this can bring freedom to their future and healing to old wounds. This is also a good time to do a quick inventory of their gifts, character, and so on.

## 2. Study Areas of Interest

As their passions and gifts are exposed and their purpose begins to surface, start to study that particular area of interest. Your son or daughter can begin to look at others who are making an impact in that arena and how they are doing it. As we have already discussed, your teens' love for this area of interest will naturally capture their attention. As they study, the details of how their purpose will be fulfilled will gradually be revealed. This is something we can encourage them to do but cannot do for them.

## 3. Find Wise Counsel

One of the best things teenagers can do is talk with people who are doing what they feel they want to do. I recommend asking several standard questions (or specific ones they come up with themselves) that will guide them in their quest:

- What is your story?
- What helped make you successful?
- If you had to do it over again, what would you do differently?
- What advice would you give someone entering the field today?
- Name a few of the key leaders in this field today.
- What are "must read" books for anyone in this field?
- What would you consider essential principles for success in this field?

- What is your next goal, and how do you plan to accomplish it?
- How does your planning process work?
- What obstacles should I look out for as I pursue this field?

### 4. Break Down Common Walls

There are walls that each of us has to face before moving to the next level in our lives. For the emerging adults in our homes, the fulfillment of their purpose is no different. As parents, we can help our teenagers prepare for their futures by helping them break through walls that stop others. We can do this by helping them develop the skills they will need for their journey. We can help them develop their character, refine their gifts, handle money, and manage their weaknesses.

## LAUNCH THEM

Kids are not in our lives as accessories. We parents have strategic roles beyond being friends or disciplinarians. We launch them into their purpose. Each year as our boys grow older, my wife gets a little emotional. She remembers when they were little and unable to do certain things. I watch her as she reminisces about the early years, and I remind her of our purpose as parents: "Just because they are really good at third grade doesn't mean they should never go to fourth." By this I mean that kids are supposed to progress. They have a greater purpose than to bring us joy. We did not design them with the gifts they possess or the purpose that burns in their hearts. We are in their lives for a season so we can prepare them for their unique greatness.

The Bible describes children as arrows in a warrior's hand (see Psalm 127:4). This is a powerful picture for parents. A warrior launches his arrows from where he currently stands in order to engage an enemy at a distance. Likewise, our sons and daughters will accomplish tasks beyond what we might imagine if we carefully prepare them and launch them in the direction of their purpose. Also, arrows are strategic weapons: each one is designed for a unique range and is aimed by the warrior with precision. As a parent, it's my job to prepare each of my kids to succeed in whatever conditions they may be facing. I am to send them out with precision and excellence in their gifts and purpose.

# 6

# From Domination to Influence: Creating an Environment for Success

We sometimes ignore the fact that parents go through a tremendous transition as their children mature. That transition begins long before the teen years. We have already talked about the difference between teaching and training. In our children's younger years, teaching took a more conscious role in our parenting. Since they come out of the womb with very few skills, we have to teach them practically everything. While we are teaching, though, we are also training them. They watch what we do and often emulate it. As our kids approach the teen years, we step out from behind our teaching podiums and come alongside them as mentors. As we walk through life with them, our emphasis will be on helping them apply what they already know.

## Dominant Versus
## Influential Parenting

From birth to seven years old, we parent by exercising our authority, or *dominating*. From our position of authority as parents, we make decisions and tell our kids what to do. When our children reach eight years old, our parenting approach should begin to change to *influential* parenting. Because these years are so crucial for our preteens and 'tweens, the smoother we can make the transition on our end the better.

Somewhere between age eight and adolescence, the transition from rule-centered leadership to principle-centered leadership should occur. We should start relying less on our position of authority and more on our influence as the most powerful voice in our children's lives. Our goal is to maintain a high level of influence from alongside them. In other words, we are no longer on the field with them showing them how to scoop up the ball "like an alligator," but on the sidelines coaching them through the game. This transition isn't easy for us because we're used to controlling the outcome of our kids' situations. We're used to winning every battle as well as the war. But if our teens are to properly develop, we will need to take on a different role.

One of the best advantages of transitioning away from rule-centered parenting is that we can allow—rather than demand—our kids to do the right thing and reap the rewards of doing so. If we never transitioned into influential parenting, they would be robbed of that growth experience.

## SHAPING VALUES, NOT JUST BEHAVIOR

Influential parenting allows us to shape not just our children's behavior but also their values. Our values are what we believe is right and wrong, good and bad, worthy and unworthy. We will stand up and fight for our values. They are based on our worldview and experiences, and they guide our lives, providing us with direction when making decisions. Values are not developed overnight, but over time, and we cannot force our children to take on our values. During different age periods, our children's value development has different areas of focus.

*Observation.* From birth until about seven years old, kids try to replicate what they see adults doing. Whatever a child experiences is taken in and considered normal and right. Children who grow up with a father who travels frequently believe that it is normal for all fathers to do that. If kids grow up watching a parent yell at the dog, they will assume it is normal to yell at the dog whenever they want the dog to do something. Whatever your children grow up watching you do will form a foundational level of values.

*Emulation.* Around age eight until about thirteen, children begin to make their own value choices. Many of the decisions they make during this phase of their value development will shape their entire lives. During this stage, our sons and daughters will also search for heroes they can emulate, internalize, and imitate. If we rely only on dominant parenting and make decisions for our kids, we will miss the boat on shaping the source of their behavior, their values. However, if we switch to a combination of rules and mentoring, we will be able to help them choose their heroes, pointing out the attributes those heroes possess that are worthy of emulating.

*Socialization.* Between ages fourteen and twenty, teenagers begin to try out their values in social settings. They will begin to take on various identities by modeling their behavior after their peers. Peer groups offer a final testing place for our kids to see how their values compare to other people's and which values they will keep.

Once our teenagers turn twenty-one, their values are basically formed. For values to change in the life of anyone twenty-one or older requires a significant emotional event.[1]

## Power to Shape

As parents, we may feel a little awkward phasing out the dominant style of parenting. But our kids are not rigid and lifeless like steel or wood; they are living and fluid in design. With that in mind, we can gain a tool to shape them that is much more user friendly in the teen years. A dominant parenting style will lose its effectiveness quickly in their preteen years. We are not talking about discipline, rules, and boundaries as much as we are talking about our position. The difference is whether we stand over them and not allow them a safe place to make decisions on their own or whether we come alongside them and put our arms around their shoulders and say, "Walk. I'm with you."

Ultimately, our goal is to give our kids freedom. As much as we would like to be involved in their adult lives, our job as parents is to raise individuals who can successfully operate independently of our control. Dr. Tim Kimmel writes, "Because you've told your children that your goal is to give them what they most want—freedom— they're less likely to demand it ahead of time. Investing more of yourself in one-on-one scenarios makes you less the person running their life and more the person grooming them for greatness."[2]

With influential parenting comes an increased ability to impact the beliefs, behaviors, and character of our teens. Parents want to instill positive beliefs in our kids so that their behavior is productive. After all, beliefs are the track our lives run on. Almost every one of our actions is inspired by what we really believe, no matter what we say. That's why behavior is such a good indicator of what someone believes. The problem with parents attempting to instill beliefs in their teenagers is that nobody can directly change another person's beliefs. For example, if I offered to pay you one hundred thousand dollars to believe right now that you are currently sitting in the White House with the president of the United States, no matter how badly you wanted the money, you couldn't believe it (unless you actually are sitting in the White House with the president). We cannot make ourselves believe something that we deeply know is false.

Teenagers already have many formed beliefs. As much as we may want to try, we cannot walk up to them, confront a belief, and demand that they change it. But we can have an impact on a belief from our position of influence. We can educate our teenagers with factual information and help them examine strong arguments against their false beliefs. Additional power to shape teenagers comes when we assume a position of influence and continue to provide boundaries and discipline as needed. My parents were masters of this. They helped shape my belief as a teenager without my even knowing it. Their strategy was dinner. Every night we came together for dinner and discussed the day's events. When a belief or action came up that was contrary to what they believed, they would shine the light of a new perspective on it and give me facts that I could use to form my own beliefs.

From a position of influence, we can effectively educate our kids. And the word *educate* means "to lead out." We can come alongside our emerging teenagers, complete with the basic skills we have implanted in them, and lead them out of ignorance toward a productive and

## TIPS FROM THE TRENCHES

*What aspects of parenting do you feel you did right?*

S. Staples: (1) We spent time with our children and regularly attended their activities, games, plays, and school events. (2) We showed them they were important and that we were interested in what they did. (3) We frequently told them we loved them, and we praised them for good work. (4) We exposed them to extended family members (grandparents, aunts, uncles, cousins) to help them see the importance of family connections and love.

C. Holland: (1) We made our kids the primary focus of our lives. (2) We spent quality time with them doing some of the things they liked.

R. Johnson: (1) We taught our kids to love the Lord. (2) We recognized the individuality of each one of our children. Sandy and I have often commented, "How in the world could the same two parents have four so different kids?"

skilled life. Several chapters in this book will give you great tips on how to maintain a close position to your teens and still be their parent.

Consider the potter and his wheel. As the potter begins shaping a beautiful creation out of a chunk of clay, he carefully knocks off large, unnecessary pieces of clay. As the wheel speeds up, the potter slowly begins applying gentle pressure and starts forming the pliable clay into whatever shape it will be. As the clay gets closer to the desired shape, the potter applies less pressure. Once the general shape

(3) We created a secure, safe environment of discipline that they could be themselves within. They learned that right decisions created right consequences, and bad decisions brought bad consequences. The way we handled each child was different, but the principles remained the same. One had to experience everything, while another would cry if you looked at them.

B. Waliszewski: (1) We had daily devotional times including my one hour of morning prayer. (2) We took a lot of family vacations together (although expensive, it's something we chose to work hard to maintain). Looking back to milestones in their lives, most people do not recall a quiet night in an easy chair, but they do often recall that trip to Hawaii or the time we went backpacking with the dogs. (3) We snow skied every winter and bought a water-ski boat when my daughter was entering high school. Those were great family bonding times!

of the creation is complete, the potter focuses on fine details to make that particular creation unique. If your child is approaching the teen years, your direct parenting has knocked off the big chunks and made a rough form of a man or woman. As you switch to indirect parenting, you will begin to make adjustments in the shape you've been forming. As your kids proceed through the teen years, you can correct mistakes and enhance fine details as your child is formed to be who he or she was created to be.

How can our kids know what's important to us without our constantly reminding them? There are some very effective ways we can lead them to do what's right. One of the most powerful methods is consistent living. Important core issues that you want to impart to your kids need to be constantly and consistently in front of them. Teen drug-use statistics back this. When parents take a strong stance of disapproval against a certain drug, use of that drug drops.

When we demonstrate beliefs and values that are important to us, our kids will grow up with a desire to uphold those values. Those standards will be normal in their view. We can help another family in need or do an act of service, and our kids will see the importance of it. When we consistently demonstrate beliefs and walk alongside our teenagers, they will be likely to consider and embrace them as their own.

Our kids will know something is valuable if we honor it. For example, not long ago my wife and I traveled to Vorkuta, Russia, to train youth workers. Vorkuta is a city just below the Arctic Circle where Stalin sent prisoners during World War II. Many of the prisoners were people who were educated and posed a threat to his regime and ideals. Amanda and I flew to Moscow first, then traveled with our team for three days by train. When we arrived in the city, we were told that men in Vorkuta were raised knowing that each time they saw one another might be the last. So they often expressed the value they had for one another by a kiss on the lips. Now, I have to admit that kissing another man wasn't in the brochure, and it caught me off guard.

But after spending a few days with these dear people, I realized why they showed such love to one another. Hearing the stories of how ten thousand of their brothers, sisters, parents, and friends were shot in a single day—and standing on the mass graves—gave me a new perspective on how these men lived. The kiss wasn't such an unusual greeting after all. Their salutation was merely one way they expressed value for one another. Likewise, when we express honor for others, our kids will model it.

As parents, we can also facilitate and fund what we believe is valuable. This is a powerful way to show kids what we feel is important. I distinctly remember my parents positioning me for success. They would never pick my friends for me. They would, however, go out of their way to put me in a circle of friends who shared values similar to those they raised me with. When I was in high school, I was in a band at my church. Every day after school I would go to church and practice or just work. My friends were there too, so we were all together having fun. Every day after school my father would come home from work, pick me up, and drive me to the church, which was about twenty-minutes from our house. I spent between thirty and forty hours per week at the church. My parents facilitated the church involvement they valued, and it paid off.

My son was playing with a friend's daughter, who is a similar age. He was overheard saying, "When we get older, we are going to get married. I really want to be a Navy SEAL, but I don't want to be away from you too long, so I will just work at Water Country" (a water park that we frequent during the summer). Choosing a mate at seven probably isn't a good idea, but I was very proud that he considered his friend so special that he wanted to marry her. By that I knew that the way my wife and I value each other, as well as the marriage we are modeling for our sons, encourages them to share those values.

In addition to facilitating activities we value, we can express our values through what we protect. When we protect our time with our spouses, our kids see the value of the marriage relationship. When we protect our nation, our kids see how much we love our country. When we protect the underdog, we teach our kids to look out for those less fortunate and to treat them right. Such values and beliefs, modeled in our daily lives, can make a deep and lasting impact.

Finally, we must never give up. When we endure hard times in our marriages, finances, educational goals, and commitments, our kids learn how to handle difficulties that they will certainly experience. I cannot recall one specific parenting tip or technique that my father has shared with me—but, let me tell you, they have been numerous. Yet every time I react to my children, I see in me what I saw in him. What he modeled for me is the exact way I am inclined to respond. When we endure hardships, we show that we value commitment, respect, and character.

When we begin to walk alongside our kids and indirectly guide them through life, we reduce the gap that exists between the facts we taught our teens and the application of those facts to their lives. We begin to help them map their course, navigate their terrain, develop their gifts, and fulfill their purpose.

# 7

# The Professional
# Role Model

There's no shortage of role models today—and there's no short-age of opinions as to what makes a good role model. "A leader knows the way, goes the way, and shows the way," says John Maxwell. "Character may be manifest in the great moments, but it is made in the small ones," says Phillips Brooks. "Resolved: never to do any-thing which I should be afraid to do if it were the last hour of my life," notes Jonathan Edwards.

And I would add that good leaders—ones worth following—accept the responsibility that comes with being a role model. But it seems that people of influence over this young generation will do any-thing but accept responsibility for their actions and behaviors. "If the parents don't like what I'm saying, they should turn it off" seems the catchy disclaimer of many of our teenagers' role models. However, with influence comes responsibility, and very few who have captured our kids' attention want to accept that responsibility and live their lives in such a way. They behave as if they can throw a disclaimer at us and not be responsible for any effects of their influence.

Yet many artists recognize the influence they have over the next generation. ("Follow me and do exactly what the song says: smoke weed, take pills, drop outta school, kill people and drink," says Eminem in his song "Role Model.") How many of these artists' children aren't allowed to hear their music or see their movies? In 2000 Madonna mentioned on *The Late Show with David Letterman* that she allows no television programming in her house. She also said that her child can watch just one age-appropriate movie per week and cartoons only if they are on DVD. Why would Madonna and other artists protect their kids from their music and other media? Because they love and care about their kids, and they know that certain music has a negative influence over those who subject themselves to it. They do not care about your children and will sell them anything.

If we want to make the maximum impact on our teens and future generations, we need to wholeheartedly embrace the idea of someone modeling his life after ours. I call it becoming a professional role model. I see a professional as someone who has intentionally become good at something. Professionals have achieved a level of mastery and are skilled at their task. I believe this generation of young people is waiting for an army of adults from all professions and walks of life to rise up and strategically position themselves as professional role models worthy of emulating. All it will take is men and women of character to come alongside them, mentor them, and help them become what they were created to be.

## What Does a Professional Role Model Look Like?

When running a relay race, one of the most crucial moments is the baton pass. The runner with the baton approaches her teammate from behind. The teammate is staring ahead, waiting for the baton to hit her fingertips. It is the responsibility of the runner carrying the baton to place it firmly in the hand of this waiting runner, because she is looking ahead, focused on the goal.

So whether you're a mom, dad, educator, counselor, mentor, youth worker, pastor, or friend, you have the baton. As you and I approach the next generation, it is our duty to successfully pass on the baton. There is no room for any disclaimers and excuses on our part as we pass our vision, values, heritage, faith, and passions on to the young men and women who will carry them to the next generation. The professional role model, realizing the importance of successfully passing the baton, lives each day waiting to put the baton in another young person's hand.

What does this professional role model look like? There is no single mold, but I can say that you don't need a Hummer, six-pack abs, a degree in adolescent development, lots of money, or success. Instead, the professional role model is characterized by a passion to reach the next generation. John Witherspoon is a great example of a professional role model. An active member of the Continental Congress, Witherspoon was the only clergyman to sign the Declaration of Independence and to ratify the federal Constitution. Those impressive credits, however, are not the only significant fruit his life produced. During his tenure as president of the College of New Jersey at Princeton, Witherspoon became a mentor to James Madison, and he influenced many leaders and thinkers as well. John Witherspoon mentored 478 young men while he served as the president of Princeton. His students went on to accomplish great things:

- One hundred fourteen became ministers.
- Thirteen were state governors.
- Three were U.S. Supreme Court judges.
- Twenty were U.S. senators.
- Thirty-three were U.S. congressmen.
- Aaron Burr Jr. became vice president of the U.S.
- James Madison became president of the U.S.
- Nine of the delegates (one-sixth) to the Constitutional Convention were College of New Jersey graduates.[1]

## THE FORMULA

Professional role models live their lives to make a great impact and embrace with excitement the opportunity they have to touch lives. There are three elements that are active in the lives of professional role models around the world. The stronger the role models are in each of these areas, the greater impact they will have on the next generation.

### Influence
The more effectual an individual's life is, the stronger the influence he or she will have on young people. These few traits can dramatically increase an adult's influence.

*Transparency.* We live in a world of fake, so it's no surprise that teens today are skeptical. They can detect something fake a mile away. But when they see someone being transparent, they know they are looking at someone who is real. This generation is like a magnet, and real is the steel that attracts them. You get the picture.

I remember watching President Clinton's impeachment hearings several years ago and being amazed as he danced around answers, refusing to simply state what had actually happened. Being transparent about what he had done would've gained him the respect of this generation, and this respect would've outweighed how offended they were by what he did. The more transparent we choose to be, the greater impact we will have on young lives.

*Authenticity.* Image is not everything; substance is. The way teenagers see things in the world is like looking at the art of Monet. From a distance, everything looks pretty, but up close it looks messy and unfocused. Teenagers will often test you to see if you are the real thing. Authenticity doesn't mean perfect. It actually means imperfect and real. My wife and I have had teens over when the house was a mess, the babies were throwing food, and the dog was running around out of control. Teens have seen us in a panic and at our worst. Yet those same kids have said, "Your family is like a fairy tale or something. I didn't know families like this really existed. I thought they were only in books." It's not that we are perfect; it's that we refuse to be fake for anyone. This generation respects genuineness.

*Consistency.* All children and teenagers need consistency. They need to know that what was right yesterday is still right today. They need to know that the boundaries don't move based on someone's mood or a change in circumstances. When consistency is lacking, teenagers will feel they need to test boundaries more: "Maybe today is one of the days Mom will let me stay out even if Dad says no." When such inconsistency is present, influence is diluted.

*Teachability.* I think teachability is one of the greatest traits a person can possess. If we are no longer teachable, we are the best we will ever be. If we seriously lack skill in a certain area but are able to be taught by someone who knows more, we will become better. Being able to take correction, especially if done with transparency in front of a teenager, is a powerful thing. I hate to pop your bubble, but they already know you are not perfect, and they know they are not perfect. When they see someone they respect take correction and change, it creates an environment conducive to positive change in them as well.

## Relationship

Professional role models, however, know that there are no shortcuts to reaching this generation. They invest their lives in teenagers by investing their time. Educators, churches, and even parents too often send messages from a distance, messages that incorporate the latest graphics and buzzwords. Yet those messages seem to have a limited impact. There are no shortcuts to reaching this young generation. They spell love T-I-M-E. More perfect words or different techniques will not impact kids as much as relationship. Relationship is the roadway into this generation. We need to first spend time preparing who we are and then prepare the roadway on which we will carry our values to the next generation.

## Clear Message

Relationships rise and fall on communication. To properly communicate with our teenagers, we need to understand them as individuals. I think of the valuable advice my father gave me when I was courting my wife. He said, "Danny, you don't have to be an expert at understanding all women. You just have to be an expert at understanding one woman." This concept applies to parenting and mentoring as well. We don't need to be experts on all teenagers, just the ones we want to impact.

As a young youth worker, I was still learning this concept. To try to get kids involved, I designed events that were revolutionary and exciting, and these events gave the teens a sense of purpose and belonging. But as the group grew, I noticed one student who just didn't seem to be in sync. I watched him over time and tried find a place where he could plug in. I learned that he was very good at golfing, so I decided to make an investment. I told him I wanted to take up golf and needed some help picking out clubs and learning to play the game. The clubs cost me about two hundred dollars, but what I reaped was invaluable. He became a very close friend who worked with me in a leadership capacity for years. He went on to earn his degree, get married, and serve on many foreign soils with Youth With A Mission. I simply learned how to speak his language and then reached out to him where he was comfortable.

In addition to knowing our target audience, we also need to communicate appropriately and consistently. What comes out of our mouths is an overflow of what's in our hearts. How we deliver those words makes a tremendous difference. When we communicate by yelling, children and teenagers naturally go into defense mode and don't hear our message. When we communicate inconsistently, we send a confusing and mixed message. We don't want to make it difficult for our kids to understand and believe us. Our communication must be clear.

When you are communicating with teenagers, remember the following simple tips.

## Teenagers Rise to Your Level of Expectation

One teenager I worked with was constantly involved in violent encounters. Terrell came into our area from a city known for violence and gang activity. He was very vocal about his allegiance to his Crip gang. Brought to our area by a family member trying to straighten him out, he was already making violent and antisocial choices. My first contact with him was during a violent encounter in a school hallway. During my entire conversation with him and his friends, I treated them with respect and dignity. Did their actions deserve it? No, but I knew that if I talked to them like thugs, they would respond like thugs. When I spoke with this young man in the same way I wanted him to act, he immediately rose to that level of expectation. In fact, in the entire time I knew him and dealt with him, he never once used profanity toward me or disrespected me. Parents would look at me in amazement as "thugs" walked into an event and "dapped me up" (affectionately greeted me). It's not as if these boys are the enemy and we should maintain an antagonistic relationship because of some of their behavior. Although I am not their peer, the proverbial cops-and-robbers mind-set does nothing but maintain walls that limit influence.

## Never, Never, Never Attack a Teen's Dignity

As I mentioned in a previous chapter, the breakdown in family structure makes gangs very appealing. When dealing with gang members, I teach school administrators and law enforcement officers to never encroach on their dignity. We each have a button, and if you are married, I'm sure you and your spouse know each other's well. Dignity is a fight-or-flight button. When a parent or teacher touches this, the teen must make a decision: either comply and lose all sense of self-respect, or walk away with self-respect intact. Teens would rather go to jail with self-respect than walk the halls of their school without it.

## Don't React; Respond

"You've ruined my life." "You are just like your father." "You are a waste of space on this planet." These are just a few comments I heard one mom make to her son, and her remarks are disturbing for a couple of reasons. First, although she meant to address his behavior, she was actually attacking her son's dignity. His behavior caused her to be angry, and she reacted out of frustration. Second, her comments didn't deal at all with the behavior she wanted to address. For example, imagine coming home to your new puppy. You walk into the house, and your puppy greets you at the door and excitedly wags his tail. As you glance up, you see that he has destroyed your couch and pillows while you were away. You get angry, the puppy sees this, but he doesn't link your anger to his destructive behavior. All he knows is that sometimes you come home mad. Whatever you do to scold the puppy may not in any way be linked to his behavior, so it will have no impact on his future behavior. This scene illustrates that reacting to misbehavior often doesn't accomplish the results we want it to.

Of course, I realize that puppies and teenagers have little in common, but when we react and say words that don't specifically deal with their behavior, the message they get is "Dad is mad again" or "I don't know why Dad hates me." When we lash out with words, we often build walls in our relationship, which compounds the teen's negative behavior. Your son hears, "You are just like your father!" and never links your anger to his behavior. He interprets your anger as "I don't like you, who you are, or who you remind me of." Although you wanted to change his behavior, the message you sent said something much worse.

And that's why it is vital that we don't react to our kids. Reacting is emotionally driven and impulsive. Dr. James Dobson writes, "There is no more ineffective method of leading human beings [of all ages] than the use of irritation and anger. Nevertheless, *most* adults rely primarily on their own emotional response to secure the cooperation of children. One teacher said on a national television program, 'I like being a professional educator, but I hate the daily task of teaching. My children are so unruly that I have to stay mad at them all the time just to control the classroom.' How utterly frustrating to be required to be mean and angry as part of a routine assignment, year in and year out. Yet many teachers (and parents) know of no other way to lead children. Believe me, it is exhausting and it doesn't work."[2]

We need to make sure we are disciplining our teens' actions and not attacking them personally. Responding means taking a step back before disciplining. If we fail to do this, we rob our kids of the consequences of their behavior, and we cause internal damage. We also set them up for a repeat performance of the very actions we want to eliminate. With foresight, though, we can plan our responses to various scenarios so we don't merely react. Our clear communication will encourage our teenagers to take responsibility for their actions and give us an opportunity to let them know we love them.

**Keep the Roadway Before the Message**
Again, the roadway into our teenagers' lives is relationship. Make the investment necessary for building that relationship. If your children are 'tweens or just entering the teen years, now is the time to beef up your relationship. Do as much as you can to bond with them and allow them to enjoy your company. Follow the lead of a woman my wife and I greatly respect. She has four sons who survived their teenage years with incredible skill. From time to time Sandy would go out and buy magazines relating to her sons' interests so she could speak their language and continue to have common ground for communication. She read sports magazines for one son and skating magazines for another. Sandy took no shortcuts in her efforts to impact her sons.

INFLUENCE + RELATIONSHIP + CLEAR MESSAGE =
GREATEST POSITIVE IMPACT

When we add these three elements together, we come up with a simple formula for impacting teens. We must have influence to be able to reach our teenagers and others around us. To be close and to be able to communicate well yet not have a life we want them to emulate is a great travesty. To have influence and communicate well with our kids without closeness is a recipe for rebellion. Take a glimpse into the life of this young man and see what I mean:

I've been taught to be a submissive dog my whole life. Obey law, obey God, obey Dad, obey Mom, obey boss, obey teacher, and so forth. There's a point where a person snaps and rebels, and goes, "I am powerful, I declare myself my own god, and I reject everything," and they go do some damage.

Closeness is essential to making a positive impact on our kids. If we have influence and closeness to our kids and do not have effective and consistent communication, the mixed message will reduce our influence and weaken our impact.

## What Are You Reproducing?

If we want to produce teenagers with character, we need to consider where we are leading them and what we are reproducing in them. Remember, we reproduce who we are, not what we know. We need to evaluate our lives. Do we react to everyone around us or are our lives built on principles? What is our worldview? Do our daily activities accurately represent our values? If we have teens or work in a capacity where we lead teens, we need to take an honest look into our own lives and ask, "Do I want to reproduce what's inside me in each of my kids?" Whether we answer yes or no, we are already on our way to reproducing ourselves. As we grow to be more like who we were created to be, we will be more comfortable with reproducing what is in us.

## Tips from the Trenches

*What are the most important lessons you've learned along the way?*

S. Staples: Kids hear what we do a lot more clearly than what we say. Patience is a virtue. Kids need and want limits, and if we provide limits in a supportive and caring way, they'll usually stay with the kids. Children need—and deserve—our time and attention.

S. Johnson: During one of the hard times we were going through with one of our sons, I learned that you can be a "perfect" parent and still have imperfect kids. That whole thinking, *If I do everything right and do it to the best of my ability, my kids will be perfect,* doesn't always apply. Another important lesson was that boys are different from girls. I grew up with all sisters. I always rejected the phrase "Boys will be boys," but that statement is true. I've talked with European, Asian, and African parents, and they have also seen how true it is. You cannot put them in a box. They are men in the making. You have to raise them flowing with the way God made them. Boys have a built-in curiosity and are daring. I would have made boys into robots who didn't object when I said, "Don't do that; you'll get hurt" or "You can't take that apart." I tried to always make things safe for my kids, but I couldn't always use my definition of safe.

## THE POWER OF PASSION

From time to time I am asked to sit in on meetings with pastors or other professionals and advise them on how to reach the under-thirty generation. In one meeting I thought about a young pastor just out of seminary who was inquiring about how he could reach his community. As we discussed different ideas, I realized that something was missing. Although this young man was equipped with many terms for various styles of ministry, there was a lack of desperation in him. He knew the talk, and he knew what he was supposed to believe, but he lacked a desire to reach the young.

When I walk down the hallway of a school and meet a young girl who feels she needs to show off her body just to be liked, I feel desperate to reach her. When I see a boy who is a walking billboard for the Insane Clown Posse, Eminem, 50 Cent, marijuana, or another antisocial practice, I feel desperate. When I see a teenager in a mall, her self-esteem so poor that she cannot make eye contact, I feel desperate.

It's time for professional role models to rise up. We can no longer be adults who read the paper and merely feel bad. And we can't sit and watch that boy walk through our neighborhood and not try to reach him. Parents, it's time to throw your excuses out the window and get a passion in your heart that says, *No matter what it takes, I will reach my daughter or my son!* When we get rid of our standard excuses for why we don't or can't do something and choose to accept the part of professional role model, we are on our way to rescuing a generation.

# Protecting the Gift and Reducing Risk

G ood morning. When you read this I'll already be dead. Yeah, it's me.... You'll find my body in the first field in front of the house.... Before you read the next page I suggest you calm down."

This is a suicide note from an eighth-grade boy. The chilling words are every parent's nightmare. Yet every day our children and teenagers are bombarded with messages that threaten their safety. As parents, we are the first line of defense to help our kids avoid the pitfalls and regrets in order to fulfill their purpose. But how do we limit the risks? As we transition to influential parenting, we begin to lose some control over the choices our kids make. Can we continue to influence them? We will discuss that and much more in this chapter.

But, first, here's my list of ten common threats our teens face every day. It's my hope that once you're aware of them, you'll be better prepared to respond to them.

## TOP THREATS

Unfortunately, I don't have enough pages in this book to adequately describe all of the threats to our teens from our culture. Some of you are well aware of what's going on, but others would be shocked to hear what even young kids are being exposed to. The fact is, you'll run into one or more of these threats during your child's 'tween and teen years, and you'll need some strategies and ammunition to both engage the enemy and empower your own principle-centered culture-changer. That's why this quick guide to the top threats confronting our sons and daughters includes some practical tips for addressing these threats in your home.

### Threat: Premarital Sex and Immodesty

"When it comes to sex, do you prefer quality or quantity?"

"What do you prefer, top or bottom?"

"Shaved or unshaved?"

"What do you think of sixty-nine?"

"Hands or tongue?"

"What do you think of sex toys?"

These shocking questions do not come from an Internet porn site. These are just some of the questions that came up in conversation between classes and made it onto a sex survey that circulated around one American high school. Students between the ages of fourteen and eighteen responded to this survey, which did not violate any of their school's conduct codes.

Our kids are being inundated with unhealthy sexual messages that warp their view of sexuality. It's not uncommon for girls to tell me that they first had oral sex in the fourth or fifth grade. We parents might read this and think that it refers to only a small proportion of kids today and certainly not to any "good kids." However, nothing could be further from the truth.

Shock and outrage can be seen on parents' faces as they peek in on a high-school dance and see what can only be described as an orgy with fully clothed teenagers. Teenagers are struggling to understand which acts are actually considered sex. Many teenagers who have engaged in oral sex consider themselves virgins.[1] Twenty-four percent of teens consider anal sex abstinent behavior.[2]

Here are a few more chilling statistics:

- One in five sexually active girls between the ages of fifteen and nineteen become pregnant each year.
- One in four sexually active teenagers will contract a sexually transmitted disease (STD).[3]
- Herpes and human papillomavirus (HPV) are now thought to affect 15 percent of the teen population. HPV has no symptoms and can cause cervical cancer when women are in their thirties.
- Girls fifteen to nineteen years old have higher rates of gonorrhea than any other age group.
- Due to the rise in oral sex, some health clinics report kids coming in thinking they have strep throat only to find out they have gonorrhea of the throat.
- Twelve thousand teens contract an STD each day.[4]
- Young women have four times the risk of contracting an STD than getting pregnant. The average pregnant teenager already has 2.3 STDs.[5]

- It is estimated that soon half of sixteen- to twenty-four-year-olds will be infected with one or more STDs.[6]
- One half of teenagers who are sexually active (orally, vaginally, or anally) have at least one of the seventy known strands of HPV.[7]

**Strategy and Ammunition**

*Move from rules to principles.* When it comes to keeping our kids pure during their teen years, rules are limited in their effectiveness. Rules say abstain from sex, while principles say protect your purity. Once we have established protective guidelines for our teens, we can begin to emphasize principle-centered purity. These principles will equip our kids to protect themselves when they are away from us.

*Teach principle-centered modesty.* From the start, mothers need to model modesty for their girls. When teaching principle-centered modesty by talking about the difference between a cheap car and a Lamborghini, I point out that Lamborghini does not advertise in cheap car magazines. In fact, that company doesn't advertise at all. The manufacturer knows that Lamborghini buyers don't care about flashy ads. In the same way, when our daughters let their inner beauty, character, spiritual strength, purpose, and principle-centered life shine, they're marketing themselves to a specific set of buyers. After all, like a Lamborghini, our daughters are made to be cherished, not used, abused, and junked. Society's standards of what is attractive does attract guys. But if our daughters want to be cherished, they need to avoid cheap marketing and cheap buyers.

*Model high expectations.* Dads, we need to limit the media voices in our sons' and daughters' lives that objectify women. Our sons need to know that they are either a protector or a predator; our daughters need to know that they are either a target or a treasure.

I've already talked about video games in which players have sex with prostitutes and beat them to death, and hip-hop artists who crudely refer to women as objects. These influences give our kids a very warped view of reality. It is never too soon to teach our boys how a man should treat a woman, and to teach our daughters how to dress and act around men and what they should expect from a gentleman.

*Equip teens with accurate facts.* The facts are on our side. Our kids need to know that:

- Most girls who get pregnant as teenagers drop out of school, and 80 percent of those girls end up living in poverty.[8]
- More women die from the effects of HPV than die from AIDS.
- Condoms do not protect against several STDs, including HPV, which can be passed on by skin contact in the genital area.[9]

Don't skew the facts. Be accurate. Sex is fun! Our kids need to anticipate sex but not be obsessed with it. Sex is not a dirty and selfish physical act, but a spiritual and bonding act that strengthens marriages and brings great enjoyment. Teaching them this fact will strengthen their desire for purity. Also remind your teens that they are dating someone else's future husband or wife.

*Protect your relationship roadway at all costs.* A pregnant fourteen-year-old will go to another fourteen-year-old girl for advice. Why? Because they have a relationship. Don't be afraid to ask tough questions to open up the roadway for communication. Create a safe atmosphere for your kids to ask anything.

*Limit negative voices.* Your teens' enemy is anyone or anything that tries to take their focus off their purpose or off the principles that are the foundation of their lives. Yes, this includes her friends and the media.

*Delay dating.* Many parents use dating age as a bargaining chip. But there's a strong reason to keep your kids from one-on-one dating as long as possible. Each year they wait, their maturity increases dramatically. Also, consider these numbers:[10]

| Age Dating Begins | Percent Who Have Sex Before Graduation |
| --- | --- |
| 12 | 91 percent |
| 13 | 56 percent |
| 14 | 53 percent |
| 15 | 40 percent |
| 16 | 20 percent |

## Tips for Talking to Your Teens About Sex

- Voice your values. Set boundaries but keep the discussion open.
- Discover your teen's gifts and purpose—and fuel them.
- Help your teens develop principles that will protect their purpose.
- Teach your kids to think. Make them wise, not just smart.
- Accentuate their positives. Teenagers need to constantly be reminded of the advantages of remaining sexually pure: (1) freedom from unwanted pregnancies and STDs, (2) freedom to love their future spouse without painful sexual memories, and (3) freedom to focus on developing their purpose and gifts.

- Look for teachable moments—and finding them in our sex-saturated society isn't difficult. At such moments, ask questions instead of making general judgmental statements.
- Don't be afraid to ask tough questions and openly discuss tough topics.
- Your teen's maturity level should dictate how much freedom he or she earns.
- Teach your teens to win early battles. It is easier to avoid sex in the early moments.
- Reduce your teen's time alone with a member of the opposite sex after certain hours. Teach your kids to never be alone with the opposite sex in a compromising situation. Encourage them to talk about boundaries early in the relationship and never cross them. One good guideline is the "three nothings": nothing below the neck, nothing lying down, and nothing taken off.
- Encourage specific and strong physical boundaries and help hold your teen accountable.

## Threat: Pornography

Pornographic material is a major contributor to divorce today. It is highly addictive. In the past the only way a teenager could look at pornography was to find it in a magazine. Today pornography has the ability to come into any room of your house through the Internet. The average age of first-time Internet exposure to porn is somewhere between five and eleven years old. Knowing that more twelve- to seventeen-year-olds use the Internet than any other age group, you probably won't be surprised to learn that 80 percent of fifteen- to seventeen-year-olds have had multiple exposures to hard-core pornography. In fact, nine out of every ten eight- to sixteen-year-olds have viewed porn online.[11] The porn industry has even ventured into the animation industry. Hentai is a form of animated pornography that many young women and men are becoming addicted to.

How big is the porn industry? The forty million adults in the United States who regularly visit Internet pornography Web sites conduct more than sixty-eight million pornographic search-engine requests (25 percent of total search-engine requests). Porn revenue is larger than the combined revenue of all professional football, baseball, and basketball franchises. The money taken in by the porn industry in the United States is more than the combined revenues of ABC, CBS, and NBC ($6.2 billion).[12]

We've already talked about other Internet threats ranging from predators in chat rooms to identity theft. Since most porn exposure is through the Internet, protecting kids from porn is similar to protecting kids from online predators. So don't hesitate to get involved in your child's cyberlife. An elementary school administrator once mentioned to me that he was dealing with a first-grade student whose personal Web page was intentionally filled with pornography. The boy stated that he'd stumbled onto a page and just started adding the images and the links. Even our youngest children are being targeted by pornographers attempting to capture their next generation of addicts. We need to make our kids difficult targets.

**Strategy and Ammunition**
*Lead by example.* Dad, if you think your kids don't know what you are viewing on your computer, you'd better think again. We need to check

our own lives and consider what we want to pass along to our kids—and that may mean getting the help we need to get free from porn.

Also, Dads, we train our daughters on what real beauty is by what we allow to attract us. If our daughters see us turning our heads at every woman who walks by, they will quickly learn what they need to do if they want to attract a guy. Men aren't the only ones attracted to pornography. Some studies indicate that one-fifth of women today struggle with pornography as well. Many adults have described to me the destruction of marriages and families caused by the unrealistic expectations and the sexual addiction resulting from involvement with pornography. The Parent and Teen Universities Inc. Web site—P-T-U.org—is a good resource.

*Install Internet filters.* Internet filtering software should be installed on every computer that has Internet access, but that technology is not completely reliable. Such software blocks only 50 percent of the porn on the Internet. Those programs work by looking for objectionable text. No software in the world can determine whether a picture is good or bad. Firewall programs and spyware programs can also help protect your computers from pornographic messages. P-T-U.org and other sites offer accountability programs that help keep Web surfers away from temptation. Their software monitors all Internet activities and sends a report to the two people you request.

*Keep computers out of bedrooms.* I recommend that no child or teen have Internet access in the bedroom. Make sure you can see who your kids are communicating with.

*Educate your teens and maintain open communication.* Our kids need to know that everyone out there in cyberspace isn't always who they say they are. When we keep the roadways of communication open, our teenagers are more likely to come to us for advice when they come across a questionable situation. Then, if we respond rather than react, we can protect our teenagers and our relationship at the same time. Let me give you an example. Johnny comes to you and says, "Mom, check this out. This guy in a chat room just sent me this picture," and what Johnny shows you is pornography. What is the gut reaction most of us would have? Ban the computer for his own protection: "We're getting rid of that thing." But if we do so, what—from Johnny's perspective—just happened? He did the right thing and was punished for it. Is it Johnny we want to punish? No. So if we don't want to train Johnny to be silent the next time, we need to reward his honesty and explain the problem.

### Other Internet Threats

*Understand predators.* During law enforcement Internet-crimes training, we went online with investigators posing as a fourteen-year-old female in a chat room. Within fifty-five *seconds* we were mailed a pornographic picture of a fifty-five-year-old woman. When pedophiles are arrested, police often find that the pedophiles have already acquired extensive databases of information. They will have children's names, cities, schools, hobbies, interests, and so on. Here's how pedophiles work: They find a child online and read his or her profile. Then they try to build a relationship with the child to gather information. They often send the child a pornographic picture and say something like, "Sorry about that. That's for big boys and girls. I didn't mean to send it to you." They immediately start to look for a crack in the parent-child relationship and exploit it. "Your dad won't let you go to the concert. That's wrong. He is very unreasonable. If you lived with me, I would let you go."

Predators will continue sending pictures, and they will either send children a Web cam to hook to the computer or ask the children to send pictures of themselves. The predator will continue driving the wedge between parent and child, even offering to send the

## THE FIRST INTERNET PARENTS

If you are the parent of a young person in the Western world today, you are unique from every generation of parents before you. You are the first parents who must be concerned with the threat of the Internet. Until recently, the biggest concern was strange-looking men in trench coats. Today, the threat is quite bigger.

*To Be or Not To Be*

"Should I allow my child to be on MySpace.com?" This is question I hear all the time, but it's merely a hint of a much larger issue. Should kids be on the Internet at all? Some parents think they'd be safest with no Internet access. But friends, technology is here to stay. Technology is a tool, like any other. A tool can save a life or take one, depending on the hands that hold it. In the hands of a relational teenager, the Internet is a

*(continued on next page)*

tool to develop and maintain relationships. Parental boundaries are required to keep that dynamic healthy.

### Let Your Teen Decide

Some teenagers haven't earned the trust to stay home alone after school, hang out with friends unsupervised, or spend an afternoon at the mall. Parents who have concerns about teens' behavior in these areas should include the online community. Teens who have proven themselves trustworthy by demonstrating proper behavior at school and in other communities can probably select good online friends as well. For these teens, MySpace could be another fun place to interact with friends. So should they be on MySpace? Your teen is the one who can answer that question.

### Make the Culture Work for You

I urge you to fully accept your role as a first-generation Internet parent. When we embrace technology, we gain unique ways to connect with our kids and strengthen these vital relationships. Technology is a huge part of our kids' lives, and embracing it means we can be influences for good in this expanding world.

### Make MySpace "OurSpace"

Get involved in your kids' Internet community. We need to teach our kids to recognize the characteristics of positive relationships and how to choose appropriate entertainment choices. Then when we involve ourselves with them in online activities, we can help them apply the same scrutiny there. When we do this, we create healthy boundaries in a crucial area of their lives. Be sure to adjust the boundaries according to the degree of trust your teen has earned.

*Trust Your Instincts*

When you have a concern about a certain activity, explain it to your teen. Remember, rules with relationship equal respect. When your teen learns to discern under your guidance, he will act safely online on his own.

*Make Your Teen a Difficult Target*

As with identity theft and similar crimes, we can become hard targets. We teach our kids to avoid certain parts of town, park in well-lit areas, and never carry their PIN with their ATM card. In the same way we need to train our teens how to be safe citizens in their online community. For example, many people fish for personal information and will steal our children's identities or worse. We must teach our kids not to give out personal information of any kind. Writing "I am Samantha from Greenbrier and I play softball" is enough information for a child predator to find her. Teach your kids about dangerous links, fraudulent e-mails, spyware, and other computer threats.

child a bus ticket. The predator may even threaten to send the pornographic pictures to the child's parents if the child won't agree to meet him in person.

It's important to know how Internet predators operate because for them, breaking the communication between parent and child is vital. We need to make sure our kids understand from an early age that, first, anyone who wants them to keep a secret from their parents is trying to hurt them and, second, that they need to tell Mom and Dad right away if they are asked to keep a secret.

### Tips About Pornography and the Internet

Is there any pornography in your home? Do you or your spouse use the Internet to look at pornographic images? Do you or your spouse watch inappropriate, sexually charged movies or television shows? read explicit romance novels with salacious covers? read questionable magazines? If so, know that your teen sees you and will likely imitate you.

So take the first step and talk with your teen about her exposure to inappropriate things. Discuss what information she should not give over the Internet. Know if she has a Web site or if she is involved in chat rooms or any other online community. I recently visited MySpace.com, a Web community, and was shocked to see inappropriate pictures of kids from my city, many of whom I knew. There were pictures of kids getting high, kids smoking marijuana, one kid holding a gun to his head, and other shocking behavior.

*Know.* Take time not only to talk to your teen but also to watch his online behavior. Does he demand privacy when online? Also view the history on your home computer and see where users are going.

Are they using file-sharing software like LimeWire or Kazaa? What kinds of pictures are they keeping on their computers? their cell phones?

*Act.* If you determine that your son or daughter is struggling with pornography, don't react. Instead respond. Your response might involve your talking with a counselor first and getting more information about the extent of use or other methods of intervention. Remember, you are the most effective weapon in dealing with porn in your child's life.

Some things you can do:

- Personally supervise your teen's online activity. This is a great opportunity to practice influential parenting by maintaining a voice in their online habits.
- Install good filtering software.
- Never have a computer with Internet access in your child's bedroom.
- Use child-friendly search engines like Ask Jeeves Kids, Google, or Yahooligans!—and have the adult-content filter turned on.
- Never assume that any software or search engine is 100 percent safe.
- Check the computer's history files regularly.
- Never reply to unsolicited e-mails or unsubscribe from lists. These actions may only be confirming that the e-mail address is in use.
- Make sure the computer is centrally located in a high-traffic area. Turn the computer monitor outward for viewing by anyone who walks by.

- Educate your kids on the positives and negatives of the Internet.
- Bookmark child-friendly Web sites.
- Instruct your kids to never give out personal information.
- Teach kids to avoid chat rooms.
- Teach kids to "crash and tell"—to immediately turn off the computer and tell a parent if a predator contacts them.
- Never allow your kids to meet someone online without your approval.
- Know the parents of your children's friends.
- User names and profiles give out a wealth of information. Consider making a family profile instead of individual ones.

Overall, teach kids to always go by these four Rs:

1. Recognize techniques used by predators.
2. Refuse requests for personal information.
3. Respond assertively if you are ever in an uncomfortable situation online.
4. Report any suspicious or potentially dangerous contact to local law enforcement.

### Threat: Music

Can music negatively impact a teenager's behavior? Neo-Nazi organizations are sure counting on it. Such hate-groups work hard to recruit the next generation through concerts featuring adrenaline-fueled "hate core" music. Many upper-middle-class teenagers flock to these events. In fact, a magazine called *Intelligence Report* reveals that hate groups have customized their recruitment pitches to frustrated Caucasian kids. One hate-group forum for recruiters had a posting that read, "We all know that music is one of our best medi-ums for reaching out to white youth with our message, so we should exploit that as much as possible."[13]

If teens are aware that music influences them, yet they still choose to listen to music that degrades women, speaks crudely about sex, and includes violent and destructive themes, they may be listening to music that crystallizes their worldview more than they are influenced by the message. We need to realize that it's not just music to them; it's an identity that they want to be associated with.

**Strategy and Ammunition**

*Teach principle-centered music selection.* Rules are helpful, but artists keep changing. So we need to help our kids navigate their lives according to their worldview and with the achievement of their pur-pose in mind. Then their music, their friends, and all the other voices in their lives will be held to the same high standard.

*Know the negative stuff.* Mom and Dad, we need to do our home-work when it comes to the media and any other sources of teen entertainment. If your teenager wants to buy a certain CD, hit the Internet. Many sites provide parents with the lyrics of each CD an artist has released. Sites like PluggedInOnline.com can also help par-ents and students make good choices in music selection. These sites are also great tools to spark discussion.

Also, beware of downloaded music. Many artists have two or three versions of the same song available. One version is what you hear on the radio, and those songs may have had the profanity taken out. But often artists have an unedited version, which is much more explicit. When kids listen to MP3s, they often download these explicit versions. Finally, beware of burned CDs. If you see a CD that's hand labeled something like "The Best of Barry Manilow," you might want to pop that into a CD player and listen to the whole thing just to be sure that's really the music on it.

*Watch for warning labels.* If the music industry determines that a CD is explicit, the packaging will contain a warning label. When the music industry says a CD is bad, it's bad. Yet many in the music industry claim that putting that little sticker on a CD boosts sales considerably.

*Be armed with facts.* What I find most troubling is the way many of these artists position themselves in front of small children to try to gain product loyalty at an early age. The movie *Shark Tale,* for example, was a who's who of hip-hop artists, many of whom have music that I could never quote in this book. From the children's programming award shows to cartoon movies, our children are being targeted. Our sons and daughters need to know that, in the eyes of the media giants, they are nothing more than a demographic to capture.

*Provide positive alternatives.* Many artists are making great sounding music with positive messages for just about every taste. Several online sources, including my Web site, are available to help you choose positive music. As parents, we should market positive music to our kids.

## Tips About Music

*Don't react; respond.* Don't start smashing CDs. Instead make an action plan for replacing the negative music with some positive.

*Focus on relationship.* Music is very important to most teenagers.

Focus on the roadway into your teenagers' lives. You could take away the CDs and win the music battle only to lose the overall war.

*Lead by example.* "Danny, I know this stuff is bad for my kids, but I really like to listen to Eminem myself." When it comes to media consumption, we must lead by example. If we choose to screen our own media to protect our focus and live according to our worldview, then we are setting a positive example.

*Have family meetings.* On my Web site and several others, media-use contracts that families can use to set tangible guidelines are available to help navigate teen entertainment. If we lord it over them when it comes to music, we may see some success when they are in our presence. But if instead we teach them to allow into their lives only those influences that support their principles and worldview, we will teach them how to make wise choices when we are not around.

### Threat: Video Games

Many top-selling video games have violent and adult themes. Some reward the players who initiate the killing and violence by exalting them to hero status. From strip shows in *BMX XXX* to killing your friends in the *Halo* series, these games can have a serious effect on kids. For whatever reasons our teens choose to spend their free time shooting people or beating women, I'm not sure there are many positive outcomes of this form of entertainment.

"Should I let my teens play video games or not?" That's the question I hear most often from parents. But it doesn't have an easy yes or no answer. Not everyone who plays violent video games becomes violent, and many kids tell me that they play "as therapy." They claim that they direct their feelings of aggression to the game instead of to real life. I struggle to fully understand that idea. These games model poor conflict-resolution skills, which could be harmful to a teenager who may already feel angry, depressed, or hopeless.

Not only can kids learn violence from a video game, but video games also desensitize them to the violence they see around them. Teenagers who engage in violent entertainment can also become more fearful and start viewing the world through a warped lens. If you allow your kids to play certain violent games, limiting the time spent on them is essential. If you see your teens becoming preoccupied with playing violent games or re-creating the pictures and scenarios, you have reason for serious concern.

Let me share some information that might spur good conversation between influential parents and their teenagers, as well as provide a foundation for the boundaries parents feel they need to set.

## Strategy and Ammunition

*Rating systems.* All video games have a rating system. Games like *Grand Theft Auto* are rated M for mature. M-rated games contain extreme gratuitous violence and very adult themes and are not recommended for any minor to play.

*Cheat codes.* Web sites give players cheat codes to video games, and some of these codes make games more gory or pornographic. Imagine buying a volleyball game for your son and finding out that he can enter a few codes and have two teams of naked cheerleaders playing against each other. *Grand Theft Auto San Andreas* has hidden pornographic material mysteriously integrated into it, and this game is marketed to kids.

*Focus.* Video games can consume our teenagers' attention. Some sources report that 14 percent of eighth and ninth graders are actually considered addicted to playing these games.[14] As I mentioned earlier, time is the greatest resource our kids have for developing their gifts and preparing to achieve their purpose. Time lost cannot be regained. Time constraints are one of the best boundaries we can offer our teenagers for any screen medium.

*Know the facts.* The fact is that high levels of exposure to violent video games has been linked to delinquent behavior, such as fighting at school and other violent criminal behavior. Nobody is immune. Research indicates that even nonaggressive teenagers are affected by brief exposures to violent video games. Teenagers who play violent video games are more likely to be involved in a violent encounter than teens who don't.[15]

**Tips for Dealing with Video Games**
- Preview any game your child plays. If the game upsets you or goes against your family's values, don't let your child play it.
- Limit the amount of time your kids are allowed to play video games.
- If your child seems preoccupied with a certain game or its theme for more than a week, talk with him about it and get help from a counselor or therapist.

## Threat: Television and Movies

The average child spends 1,248 hours watching television and only nine hundred hours in school each year. With the amount of time teenagers are spending in front of screen media, the messages they receive are crucial to consider. According to the American Psychiatric Association, by age eighteen, an American youth will have seen sixteen thousand simulated murders and two hundred thousand acts of violence. A study conducted by RAND and published in the September 2004 issue of *Pediatrics* looked at 1,792 teenagers between the ages of twelve and seventeen and determined that those who watched more sexual content were twice as likely to begin having sexual intercourse and advancing to other sexual activities.[16]

### Strategies and Ammunition

*Know what's on.* Television skews perceptions of reality for many teenagers. Encourage your teens to make decisions about what they watch based on their principles and values. Also help them realize that television can impede their ability to attain their potential. To limit exposure to destructive voices that MTV and other programming may bring, you may have to take some serious steps. Carefully choose cable packages. Visit Web sites like ParentsTV.org that can give you accurate information about what's on. You can also sign up for e-mail lists with timely information like the one Parent and Teen Universities Inc. (P-T-U.org) provides.

*Set boundaries.* Establish consistent boundaries to keep your teenagers safe. Set time limits and select programs that don't contain negative influences. I recommend that no child have cable programming in his or her bedroom. Remember that MTV, HBO, and other similar stations often have nearly pornographic material on them certain hours of the day. Some filtering programs for television are helpful as well. Take advantage of satellite and cable locking and blocking features, but don't totally rely on them.

*Beware of ratings.* Most parents think a PG-13 movie is like *Finding Nemo* with a couple of mild profanities thrown in. Nothing could be further from the truth. Typically, movie producers will take their films to the ratings committee and ask, "What needs to be taken out to bring this movie down to PG-13?" The committee will advise them which scenes to drop or which profanities to remove. Many "teen movies" are just barely below R-rated.

*Be aware of theater jumping.* Fellow youth speaker and good friend Phil Chalmers and I rarely go to see movies. There are many reliable sources to study without subjecting ourselves to the filth aimed at teens. But when *American Wedding* came out, we knew that we needed to be familiar with it, since both of us speak to thousands of kids each year about media influences. At first there were very few teenagers in the theater. Ten minutes into the film, they started to enter two by two. Soon there were at least sixty underage teenagers watching this movie. After talking with some of them, we figured out that they had purchased *Finding Nemo* tickets but jumped over to the *American Wedding* theater. This practice is quite common for teenagers.

*Make your teens wise.* It's very important for our teenagers to learn how to navigate their culture using principles that will help them fulfill their purpose, no matter what negative influences surround them. A parent's rules set good boundaries, but the principles we help our teens establish will keep them making good decisions on their own.

### Tips for Dealing with Television and Movies

The American Academy of Pediatrics (AAP) offers the following practical recommendations about television habits in homes.

1. Start talking to your kids while they are young about the television programs, movies, and other media they use.

2. Set television rules for the family, as a family.

3. Put your family on a healthy television diet, creating balanced "TV meals" with your children. Look for television programs with nutritious messages and role models. Educational programs count. An occasional TV snack or dessert—a program watched for entertainment or relaxation alone—may be all right, but they should come after the main course and not dominate the diet.

4. Your family television diet will be most successful when accompanied by activities. According to the AAP, "TV programs should be springboards that spur curiosity, discussion, and learning." For example, ask your kids questions about what they learned from watching the program or what they like or don't like about the characters.

5. Teach your teens how to critically view the media they watch, so they can see motives, techniques, and agendas. This is an essential goal of influential parenting.

6. Whenever possible, watch television with your teenager. It will provide numerous teachable moments.[17]

## Threat: Drugs and Alcohol

According to the graduating class of 2005, we have reason to be concerned about alcohol and drug use. Over 70 percent of them reported that they abused alcohol, and 34 percent used marijuana in the past year.[18] Studies also indicate that nearly half (47 percent) of today's eighth graders have experimented with alcohol.[19]

Why do kids use drugs? To prepare for youth drug-prevention training for law enforcement agencies, educators, and parents that I conduct across America, I interviewed teenagers who were abusing illegal drugs. I wanted to gain some insight as to why they started and continued to do something that most agreed was harmful to them. I was surprised by their answers. Here's what I learned:

*Reason 1: community.* Overwhelmingly, teens tell me that they use drugs because that's the community they fit into. The drug community accepts everyone. You don't have to be a size zero, bench-press three hundred and two pounds, drive a nice car, or have lots of money to be accepted. And as you have read, relationships are everything to teenagers.

*Reason 2: to numb pain.* Almost without exception, teenagers involved in the drug culture have given up hope of fulfilling their dream or life's purpose. Many of them know tremendous pain caused by a broken home, abuse, rejection, or some other issue. Yet many drug-prevention campaigns focus on how drug use will destroy lives. First, that assertion contradicts one of the most powerful forces in teenagers' lives: their experience. They say, "I smoke weed. I feel better. Period." Second, those teens already feel that their lives are ruined. How could drugs make it worse? In their view, drugs help them cope with pain.

But drug abuse is slow suicide. Most regular drug users I have talked to simply exist with no hope of doing anything better for the rest of their lives. Incidentally, I believe this is why drug use is declining among teenagers.

*Reason 3: parental training.* Parents who use chemicals to change the way they feel often impart that technique of relaxation, recreation, and conflict resolution to their children. Many teen users I talk to admit that their parents also abuse illegal chemicals and that they quite often do so more than the teens do.

*Reason 4: peer pressure.* A smaller number of teens than might be expected say that they have been pressured into using drugs and alcohol. In most of those instances, the teens were in a place of transition in their development and trying various circles of friends. Some felt pressured by a friend who was on the fringe of the drug crowd. Most of the peer pressure experienced comes from circles of influence that students choose, making it close to reason 1.

### Teen User Facts

Teenagers have some unique attributes when abusing chemicals. First, it's not uncommon for them to take several drugs at the same time. Cigarettes, alcohol, and marijuana are not gateway drugs, but gateway experiences. Teenagers ingest just about anything to change how they feel, in hopes of feeling some kind of new experience.

Second, teen users don't understand dosage. How many drinks are in a forty-ounce beer? Most chemical-abusing teenagers will answer, "One." Many teenagers are taking over-the-counter cold medications to feel drunk or take away pain. These teens tell me that they steal these products and take the entire box or bottle at once. And without considering the possible consequences, they will mix and match products to try to get a better high.

Finally, adult alcoholics may have two or three people in their lives who will lie or cover up for them. But a teenage chemical abuser may have between *forty* and *fifty* enablers. Teens will keep a friend's struggle with addiction secret to protect the friendship.

*Which drugs are teens abusing?* Drugs of abuse for 'tweens and teens are constantly changing both nationally and regionally. In some regions methamphetamine is more accessible than other drugs. In certain seasons, marijuana doesn't grow well, so psychedelic mushrooms, or shrooms, will be used. Cigarettes and alcohol are highly abused too, and here are a few of the other chemicals kids are choosing.

*Marijuana.* Roughly 80 percent of all drug abuse is marijuana.[20]

*Inhalants.* Anything that smells strong can have an effect on the brain, so kids will often inhale substances to feel high or see stars. Such inhalants are among the deadliest chemicals of abuse that kids experiment with. While most other drug use is declining, inhalants seem to be gaining popularity, especially with middle schoolers. Kids will use Freon from an air conditioner, markers, spray paint (usually metallic colors that will be visible around their mouths and noses), glue, and anything else that smells strong. Several years ago two middle-school girls at a sleepover thought they would be able to see stars if they sprayed room deodorizer into a towel and held it to their faces. Their bodies were found in the morning. Inhaling is deadly.

*Over-the-counter drugs.* Many teenagers, especially middle schoolers, will take over-the-counter pills and products. Many products taken in high quantity cause effects similar to LSD.

*Prescription pills.* Kids abuse many pills that are prescribed for parents and grandparents. Some of them, such as OxyContin, are excellent painkillers, but when the pills are crushed, the drug becomes more potent than heroin.

Kids are also experimenting with club drugs, such as Ecstasy and others. They are also moving into methamphetamine, cocaine, and heroin. With these changing trends come changing indicators.

**Indicators**

What I am about to share with you is based on both my personal experience working with kids and my research with drug-using teenagers. Law enforcement calls signs of possible drug use "indicators." The more indicators in a teen's life, the more likely that teen is trying to associate with the drug community. Although indicators don't specifically mean the student is using a certain drug, strong indicators are a reason for concern.

Also, indicators are different for all types of groups that teenagers join. Let's look at the marijuana group as an example. Marijuana users may be fascinated with marijuana art, including drawing marijuana leaves on their papers, books, and even their backpacks using Wite-Out. They may also like psychedelic images, including mushroom and LSD art. They may write "420" on their property, which is known as the international time to smoke marijuana. They will wear hemp necklaces, patchouli oil for cologne, or even small mushroom artwork that represents psychedelic mushrooms. They will probably want to listen to music synonymous with the drug community. Kids who advertise that they listen to Led Zeppelin, The Grateful Dead, or Jimi Hendrix are probably not simply connecting with your roots, Mom and Dad. Phish and other bands also have a large following of drug users. And many reggae, hip-hop, and rap artists actively promote drug use. If your kids are choosing to listen to these artists, consider why.

Another drug that is popular with this generation is Ecstasy, which also has its own culture and indicators. Items associated with Ecstasy use include glow sticks, flashing lights, Vicks VapoRub, surgical masks, pacifiers, and techno music. All of these items affect how much fun a user has while under the influence of the drug. Unfortunately, the massive increase in Ecstasy use has caused many of the items used by Ecstasy users to become popular among Millennial kids. Just because your son or daughter wants a glow necklace certainly doesn't indicate an association with a drug culture, but numerous indicators might merit some concern.

### Strategies and Ammunition

*Circle of influence.* You may not be able to choose your teens' friends, but the wider the circle they have to choose from, the better.

*Dream check.* When teens have a clear understanding of what they are doing and where they are going in life, they will gain hope and purpose. This is the most powerful way parents can help their kids avoid drugs. Dreams truly are the best antidrug.

*Emotional effects.* Emotions are like muscles. When we are young, we go through difficult experiences and we grow emotionally strong. If a teenager takes a chemical when life gets difficult, what will he do when he's thirty-two years old and receives a pink slip? If he has a house payment and two kids to feed, he can't go home and get high until circumstances get better. It is vital that we don't allow our kids to take any chemicals unless prescribed by a physician.

*Model.* When we model responsible behavior with chemicals, we train our kids how to handle chemicals in their own lives. When our kids see us walk through difficulties without turning to a bottle, pipe, or pill, we are shaping that generation's behavior.

*Create safe risks.* Teenagers need safe opportunities to spread their wings and take risks. When they participate in activities, such as white-water rafting, scuba diving, mountain climbing, mission trips, and so on, they gain a personal sense of accomplishment and demonstrate independence and inner strength. If you have a son, you have a warrior looking for a battle to win, a knight wanting to rescue a princess. We channel this unbridled passion when we provide our teens with acceptable outlets.

**Behavioral Indicators of Drug Use**
- physical symptoms
- unusual defensiveness
- secrets (more than usual)
- withdrawal from family
- change in friends
- falling grades
- dropping long-term interests
- change in hygiene
- change in the way they dress

## *Threat: Violence and Gangs*

Kids turn to gangs for several reasons. With the destruction of families, more and more teenagers are turning to gangs to find their sense of belonging and relationship. Many kids are attracted to gangs by the opposite sex, drugs, or parties. Some teenagers gain a sense of self-respect or power. Many young people find a sense of family in their gang. Money, protection, and real or perceived family problems may all make kids feel more comfortable on the street.

There are many indicators that your son or daughter may be associating with a gang. You should, of course, be concerned if your teenager admits to being in a gang or is obsessed with a particular color of clothing. Colors have meaning to most gangs. For example, a black T-shirt often means that a teenager is associating with a gang but has not yet been "beat in" and allowed to wear the color of the gang. Gang members may wear a white shirt with a colored hat or bandanna. The bandanna represents the gang, and the white T-shirt says they have no beef with another gang. Members of a gang may also wear excessive jewelry with distinctive designs, or they may wear jewelry on a certain side of their body. Most gang members are obsessed with gangster-influenced music, videos, and movies to the point of imitating characters. You may also notice them withdrawing from family and gaining a new antisocial attitude, breaking parental rules, and hanging with unapproved friends. With that may come a new need for privacy and secrecy as well as the practicing or exchanging of hand signs or handshakes. If you see evidence of physical injury and are told lies about how the injuries happened, unexplained cash or clothing, or new drawings or tattoos, you may have a reason for concern.

**Nontraditional Groups and Gangs**
Legal definitions of gangs vary by state. Most agree that a group of individuals with a name and colors who commit crimes is a gang. Most youth violence is group or gang related. That's why your teen's circle of influence and friend selection are vital to the ability to avoid destructive choices. Remember, if you can show me your teen's friends, I can show you his or her future. Providing positive environments and influences is also absolutely essential.

**Tips for Dealing with Gangs and Violence**

- *Recognize the signs.* Know the indicators of violence and gang involvement.
- *Spend time with your teenagers.* They need you now more than ever.
- *Empower your teens.* Are they being distracted from developing their gifts and fulfilling their purpose? From your position of influence, you can help them make the right choices.
- *Don't ignore rules.* Rules are the guardrails of our teens' lives. Set and enforce protective boundaries.
- *Allow consequences.* Teenagers need to experience the consequences of their behavior. The earlier they do so, the more likely they will be to make corrections and new choices.
- *Be a role model.* Make sure you are leading your kids by your example.

## *Threat: Suicide and Cutting*

In almost every school I speak at, some of the students tell me that they are considering suicide. In one church youth group I spoke at, more than fifty kids raised their hands when I asked if they had considered or were currently considering suicide.

Suicide isn't the only thing going through their minds. Unlike suicide, self-injury is done to cope with life instead of end it. After speaking at a middle school, I got the following e-mail from a desperate young woman:

Hello Mr. Danny…lately I've been very depressed about
school, home and my family. It just seems like everything is

going wrong.... I never want to eat anything anymore. I'm always tired and feeling hopelessness. I've been cutting myself for about a half a year now. I think it's the only way to help me through this.... I feel like I want to do more than cutting—going further. And not looking back. Just going all the way until I'm gone from here.... Please help me before I do something permanent about my situation.

This young woman is involved in a serious, life-threatening situation. Her self-injury isn't limited to cutting; it also includes not eating. She is crying out for help. Don't minimize the seriousness of such symptoms if you see them in teenagers in your home or circle of influence. Remember: suicide is a permanent solution to a temporary problem.

### Tips About Suicide and Cutting

*Watch for warning signs. If you see any, get help immediately.* Warning signs are changes in behavior, feelings, or beliefs that last two weeks or longer and seem to be uncharacteristic of an individual. Here are some early warning signs:
- difficulties in job or school
- talking about suicide or death
- depression
- neglect of appearance
- increased substance use
- dropping out of activities
- changes in sleeping habits
- isolating oneself from others

- feeling that life is meaningless
- loss of interest in activities
- a sense of hopelessness
- restlessness and agitation
- displaying helplessness

Here are some late warning signs:

- feelings of failure
- sudden improvement in mood
- overreaction to criticism
- preoccupation with one's failures
- overly self-critical
- collecting means to kill oneself
- anger and rage
- having a suicide plan
- making final arrangements
- pessimism about life, the future
- ending significant relationships
- giving away possessions
- an inability to concentrate
- preoccupation with death
- taking unnecessary risks[21]

## THE BEAUTY OF GUARDRAILS

As a youth worker, I've taken a number of trips with teenagers. One of the most memorable was when I took them to the New River Gorge in West Virginia. As awesome as it was to go down class IV rapids and hang off a cliff hundreds of feet above the ground, the most hair-raising experience of the trip for me was the van ride! If you have ever driven a van with fifteen screaming teenagers over the mountainous terrain of West Virginia, there are some things you need to know.

First, you should carefully read the road signs. On the back roads of West Virginia, the signs are custom-made. They're nothing like what you could buy at the local sign shop. Second, you really should observe the speed limits. When signs say "Speed Limit 7 MPH," they do not mean ten miles per hour. In fact, they must assume everyone is driving a Porsche 911, not a van. The only time I was remotely comfortable driving those roads with a dozen or more lives in my hands was when I saw a guardrail.

Mom and Dad, pay attention here. The guardrail meant one thing to me: on the other side of that piece of metal was something very dangerous, but the rail was there to protect me. From the driver's seat I could see down the steep ravine, so when that guardrail ended, I got very nervous.

Structure and rules are like guardrails. As teens navigate the mountain road of life, they see many road signs. Teachers, coaches, parents, youth pastors, mentors, and others are holding signs. The signs read, "Have fun on the road of life, but watch out for _____." Sure, sometimes teens think seven miles per hour really isn't for them. Sometimes they ignore the signs you're holding up: Stop. Save Sex for Marriage. Stop. Don't Lie. Stop. Smoking Will Kill You. Stop. Pick Your Friends More Wisely. Sometimes they will crash, and you'll spend time picking gravel out of their wounds. But the guardrails are a comfort nevertheless.

And kids who control their homes, those who do whatever they want without any consequences, are calling out for someone to set up a guardrail. They are screaming, "Mom, please stop me from doing drugs. Please tell me that I can't hang out with my friends. I know I'll argue with you, but deep down inside I will know you love me, care about me, and want to protect me." I've heard kids boast about parents who let them do whatever they wanted or brag about how they moved into Dad's place because he let them drink with their friends. But these kids usually had the most regrets, fewest true friends, greatest pain, and worst behavior as they cried out for attention. Overall, they were the unhappiest kids I've worked with. Teenagers with no boundaries are often very unsure of where they are in life and the risks they are taking. They are less secure during a time of life when they need the security of parental care more than ever.

On the other hand, the kids I work with whose parents set rules have the most fun and are the most productive kids around. Your teens may complain about the rules you set, but inside they know that you care about them and that it's safe to have fun within those boundaries.

Consistent discipline and rules within the context of a solid relationship with your teenager offer a powerful deterrent against destructive decisions and allows kids to enjoy life more.

One more thing, Mom and Dad. Remember when you were a kid and all of society frowned on destructive behavior? Everywhere you turned there were influences that pointed you in the right direction. Children today don't have that luxury. So if you don't actively plant values into the soil early and if you don't consistently pull the weeds, you will find unhealthy and dangerous things taking root in their lives.

## PRINCIPLES—THE FOUNDATION

What happens when we are not there to hold up a street sign or put up a guardrail? When our teens are at a friend's house watching movies, messing around on the Internet, listening to music, or hanging out, what can we do to help them make right decisions? There is something, combined with rules, that protects our kids very well, and that something is *principles*. Principles don't replace the protective boundaries of rules; they provide the foundation for *why* the rule is in place. To establish principles in our kids, we need to get "Because I said so" behind us. Principles can serve as a navigation system that helps our kids get to their destination without our step-by-step directions.

There are some traits about principles that are foundational and vital to know. When making decisions, people are generally proactive or reactive. Proactive people focus on what they can control, and they make decisions based on their values and where they want to end up in life. Proactive people write their own scripts, and their internal principles guide their behavior. On the other hand, reactive people hand the scripts of their lives over to others and are controlled by outside influences.

As we help our teenagers discover their gifts and purpose, we can also help them develop the principles they will use to take control of their lives so they won't haphazardly surrender to whoever is on the screen, in the headphones, or at the party. Our kids will learn that they are responsible for matching their behavior to their principles.

I believe the only way our society will reverse some of its tasteless and degrading trends is for solid teenagers to take their role as leaders, equipped with solid principles and convictions, and attack negative culture head-on. Everyone has influence, including our kids. We need to raise them to be more than just smart; they need to be wise.

## WORLDVIEW

The battleground is in our worldview. If we want our kids to make right choices, we need to shape them at their core—their worldview. If teenagers have a solid worldview, built on accurate facts and solid principles, they will be less influenced by harmful entertainment, and they'll have less desire for it. We don't need to tell our kids that songs about raping women, slitting throats, and having sex with corpses are bad influences. We need to train them to understand the source of their actions and identify their destination in life.

In order for your teenagers to develop their worldview, they need to answer four questions:

1. Where did I come from?
2. What is the purpose of life?
3. How should I live?
4. Where am I going?

The answers to these four questions comprise a worldview. Teenagers then need to write a script for their lives based on principles that they establish from that view. They may have a worldview centered on their faith in God and view themselves as eternal beings created for His purpose. If that is the case, their principles for how to live life will reflect that purpose.

From there they will choose the influences in their lives. Rules

## TIPS FROM THE TRENCHES

*Name one of the most important character traits you wanted to pass along to your teens.*

S. Staples: Responsibility for their own actions and outcomes.

C. Holland: Character and worth. Who you are is more important than what you do, but you can do anything you set your mind to do.

R. Johnson: Generosity. So much stems out of that.

S. Johnson: Making choices the right way morally. You pay now or you pay later.

B. Waliszewski: Living a life of no regrets, full of integrity.

*Were you successful? If so, what was your approach?*

S. Staples: I think so. We often reinforced the idea that *we* create our own environment even if we don't control everything. When the girls were frustrated with things they couldn't control, we pointed out what they did control and encouraged them to deal with those things. We also gave them opportunities to show responsibility at home.

R. Johnson: Yes…We fundamentally reproduce who we are. After all the talk, we still genuinely reproduce who we are. I think the things I see in their lives that concern me are the things I see most in my own life. I think understanding yourself and teaching yourself to be a right person goes a long way in producing good kids.

are not needed nearly as often for a principle-centered teenager as they are for teens who are trying to follow a script of rules provided by someone else in a world they are constantly reacting to. Any battle-scarred veteran will tell you that battle plans are good for the first ten minutes of a battle, and then leadership takes over. Battlefield leaders adapt fluidly to rapidly changing conditions. When we ground our teenagers in principles, no matter what the newest threat is, they will skillfully take what they know and deal with it.

## CREATIVE PARENTING—CREATING SAFE RISKS

Our older son, Josh, likes to take risks. We could see it coming last summer. It's really my fault. I was speaking at a large conference for educators in Anaheim, California, and I found the most incredible gift in the exhibit hall: a bug-catching kit. Recalling the joy of catching fireflies and other critters when I was younger, I thought my boys would love a kit. It would encourage them to venture outdoors for some memory building.

One day seven-year-old Josh exploded through the front door, bug-catcher kit in hand. We should have known that something was definitely afoot when his eyes were as big as saucers. "Mom, check this out!" His momentum carried the projectile within inches of my wife's face.

"What is it?" Amanda calmly asked.

"It's a widow," he panted.

"A *what?*" asked Amanda.

"It's a black widow!" Josh exclaimed. I can assure you that it was only polite disbelief that inspired Amanda to take the flimsy container and hold it above her head for a quick inspection. I didn't realize she was capable of moving as quickly as she did toward the door. It was true. Josh had found a female black widow spider and coaxed it into his kit.

---

*To enjoy the things we ought and to hate the things we ought has the greatest bearing on excellence of character.*

—ARISTOTLE

---

Proud father that I was, I wanted to say, "You go, boy!" and affirm this milestone experience as a rite of passage, but the lingering memory of an episode of Animal Planet's *Venom ER* seemed to take over my mind. As much as I want my sons to grow up with a sense of accomplishment, I want the risks to be less harmful than being injected with venom that is fifteen times more toxic than a prairie rattlesnake. There's got to be a better option.

Teenagers' brains are being hard-wired and constructed until the time they approach their midtwenties. As kids exercise their brains and learn to deal with thoughts and impulses, they lay foundations that will last the rest of their lives. When we help our teenagers establish principles for life and come alongside them as influential parents, they learn skills they will use their entire lives. Do we want to hard-wire that brain for sitting in front of a screen for up to eight hours per day? The trick is finding creative and safe stimulation for them. With the experimental nature of teenagers, safe risks are not always available, so often teenagers will venture into drugs, alcohol, sex, and crime. If your teens are starting to venture into risky areas, you may need to find or create safe opportunities for them to venture out and establish their identity. Camps, trips, and many other opportunities are available, but you will need to find the right one for your son or daughter. As Ted Haggard and John Bolin say in *Confident Parents, Exceptional Teens,* "It takes forty acres to raise a child."[22]

After school one day I was contacted by a teenager who had some troubling news. While on the way home from work that afternoon, his father had been involved in a fatal accident. I immediately went to the house to be with the family. While talking to the teenage son, I asked him about his father and some of the special moments he will remember forever. One after another, stories began to flow from him. As he talked about scuba diving in the Cayman Islands and various other physical activities, I could tell that the teenagers in this family were raised by parents who were very active in their lives and who structured their priorities around enjoying and developing their kids. Many great memories are made when our families share outdoor activities. And at the same time the influence of screen media and other negative entertainment is reduced. It's a win-win situation for parents—and for their teens!

# Part III

# PRACTICAL PRINCIPLES EVERY PARENT NEEDS TO KNOW

Nice to meet you. I'm not likely to cross the line into killer territory, at least while [I'm] young. Once you're an old man and got nothing to lose…. I suppose you could take my words for a lot of teens. I think the biggest problem is not necessarily being picked on, but how people deal with it. The people that are beaten on have no real ability to have any personal recourse. Going to a teacher or cop makes you feel weak. People call you a rat. If you decide to go just upfront and bash the guy, well, you get in ***** too, and unless you're willing to lose everything, most people simply suck it up and repress their feelings. Basically, everyone tells you, "Violence isn't the answer," and I ask, "Well, what is the answer?" They spit out morals and being "better" than the other person. They tell you to punch a pillow or write a cheap, angsty teen poem. These methods just don't work…. Life caters to those who are willing to throw down the social rules, and accept that evil can prevail just as much or more than good. I accept that good and evil are relative to the individual, and that there is no universal standard for what's right and wrong (at least not apparently). So now, why bother with cops...and teachers to deal with my problems when I can smile at the ***** bugging me, knowing I'm going to burn his house down, severely damage his things, possibly kill his precious pets, and basically stab him in any way I can without even telling him? That's the only option people are really left with. It just takes awhile for people to get there, after constantly being depressed, kicked, and no one truly caring.

—TEENAGER, e-mail correspondence

# The Connection:
# Building and Maintaining
# Healthy Relationships

It's many a young man's dream to grow up close to the beach, and I lived that dream. I grew up living within an hour and a half of Nags Head, North Carolina, home of some of the best beaches on the East Coast. There is nothing like driving your Jeep with the top down on the sand right along the ocean's shore. Recently, my wife and I strapped the boys in the Jeep Rubicon with the top down and drove down to Nags Head and out onto the beach. The long ride was forgotten in the fun and excitement we had playing in the sand and ocean. In 2003, though, we experienced another aspect of living near the coast. Hurricane Isabel hit the Nags Head area directly with great force. Even living one hundred fifty miles away we felt the pounding of the storm and lost power for a week.

As wonderful as Nags Head is when it's not hurricane season, it does have one serious flaw. Even though thousands of families visit Nags Head each week, there is only one main road in and out of the area. When storms come, traffic can be backed up for dozens of miles as people try to escape the potential fury. The same highway that is a route to great pleasure is also the only way of escape.

## PASSIONATE DESPERATION TO CONNECT

Parents, relationships are the roadway into our teenagers' lives. We cannot rely on mere biology to carry us through. We cannot say, "I'm your mother. You will listen to me!" and expect our kids to positively respond. We need to be motivated by a passionate desperation to connect with our teens. When we say, "No matter what it takes, I will connect with my son," then we're on our way. Desperation forces us to do whatever needs to be done to reach our teens. Desperation forces us to go where we are uncomfortable going so we can connect.

Many times we adults want our communication to produce a result. We want our teens to bring up their grades, get better friends, stop their negative behavior, and so on. We look at other families whose kids are perfect little angels and compare them to ours. This exercise is neither productive nor accurate. Every family is unique, with unique strengths and weaknesses. When we are consumed with what we cannot change or areas we feel are weaknesses, we risk losing valuable time that could be spent on refining what is strong and effective in our families. When we react to things we cannot change, we make our families unstable and controlled by others. When we center our families on the principles that are most important in our lives, we take control of our homes and write the script that is perfect for us.

---

*And so I wasn't there to see him as he began to sink into himself. I wasn't there to sense, even if I could have sensed it, that he might be drifting toward that unimaginable realm of fantasy and isolation that it would take nearly thirty years to recognize.*

—LIONEL DAHMER, father of serial killer Jeffrey Dahmer
  writing about his lifestyle that kept him too busy to be
  involved with his son.[1]

---

Though we may have a better sense from our parental perspective than our kids do of what's at stake in their actions, our teenagers are not concerned with the result our talk with them will produce. Often they are more concerned with their relationship with us. Occasionally when I discipline my own children, I can see in their faces when they have the greatest feeling of regret. It usually isn't when a privilege or object is taken away but when they feel they have disappointed me. This intense desire for connection with parents is something we need to protect and strengthen as our children grow up. When our teens know they are more valuable to us than our friends, our reputations, and our careers, they will attempt to maintain that place of honor in our lives.

Maybe you are struggling with your relationship with your teenager. You may need to communicate vital information, but when you talk, your teen hears none of it. If your message isn't getting across—if all your teen hears is the voice of Charlie Brown's teacher, "Wah wah wah wah wah wah," that's not an instruction problem, that's a relationship problem. Something has blocked the roadway into your son's or daughter's life, and it is absolutely essential that the path be reopened. If your relationship with your 'tween or teen is already strong, keep the roadway open and clear. A crisis is no time to build a relationship. The time to build is now, and here are some steps you can take to do so.

## FOUR RS OF CONNECTING

While studying for youth work, I was taught the four Rs of communicating with this young generation outlined in Tim Celek and Dieter Zander's *Inside the Soul of a New Generation*.[2] Whether or not these four traits are present can make or break communication with our kids. Let's take a look at them now.

### Real

This generation is in love with things that are real. They have been bombarded with fake, and they can detect it easily and quickly. It is, therefore, a huge misconception that today's kids believe everything they hear. They don't. Just about every institution in our culture has lied to them. So they trust what they experience. If people are innocent until proven guilty, this generation would consider most sources of input fake until proven real. No matter how moving the attempt by politicians to capture the allegiance of this generation, these young people sense fake, assuming that hidden agendas are at work. This is why many young people turn to *The Daily Show* and *Letterman* for an interpretation of "what was really said." From religious leaders abusing children to a growing social security crisis, they are watching and trusting less and less. They tend to respect people who are authentic, even if the authentic picture is less than perfect.

Consequently, if we want to be able to communicate with our sons and daughters, it is vital that we are real with them. We need to be "raw" in our communication. We need to avoid fancy words and complex thoughts; we just need to tell them the truth. Our communication must be vulnerable, transparent, and imperfect. We don't need to tell our kids all the dirt from our past, but neither do we want to paint an unrealistic picture of perfection. Kids sense the truth, and being anything but honest and real is fatal to communication.

Nothing brings this truth to light better than the research that was done on the drug Ecstasy. Some time ago national studies stated that there were holes in a brain under the influence of Ecstasy, and kids were told that one recreational use would cause permanent damage. Several years later, however, further research indicated flaws in the research from Johns Hopkins University. Initial researchers have now admitted that they accidentally used methamphetamine instead of Ecstasy in the study. While blame is still being thrown around, let's look at this situation from our kids' perspective. Our kids were lied to about the dangers of a drug. The best credentials in the world are worthless to them if the people holding those credentials can't be trusted. If teens feel betrayed and lied to, they will disregard all information from that source—accurate or false. Being real with teens makes such a predicament a nonissue.

Being real in our relationships with our sons and daughters has another powerful advantage. When we are real, we take the first risk. When we take the initial risk in a conversation or relationship, we are sowing a seed of trust. In their minds, our teens are saying, *I could hurt Mom with my words right now because she just trusted me with something. But since she did trust me, maybe it's safe for me to trust her.*

When I'm speaking to teenagers, I will occasionally tell a story specifically to develop their trust. It's about my orthodontics experience, which wasn't pretty. You see, when I was a young teen, I had terrible teeth. I literally had one of my bottom teeth growing under my tongue, and it would have come out of my chin had it stayed in there. After oral surgery I got braces. I remember the day I went to get the braces taken off. I was thinking, *Danny, now girls are gonna like you.* I sat in the chair running my tongue along my smooth teeth and dreaming of the next day at school. My dad and the orthodontist, who will remain unnamed, walked around a little half wall to have a private conversation. "Well, Mr. Holland, we took care of his teeth. Now all we have to do is take care of his face." (Did I mention I had a pretty severe case of acne?)

When I tell this part of the story, students almost always react because they are identifying with me. Then I go on with the story. "As you could imagine, the ride home was quiet. My dad said, 'Danny, the doctor gave me the number of a doctor who can look at your skin.' Sure enough, I went to the dermatologist and had a zit exam. He popped one, looked at it under a microscope, and said, 'Danny, I have good news. There is a pill that can take away your acne.' Good skin *and* good teeth? I'd be a babe magnet! Sensing my enthusiasm, the doctor said, 'But there is one side effect. It causes severely bad body odor.'" At this point in the story, I pause. I usually have a thousand or more faces staring back at me as if to say, "Danny, what did you do?" I finish the story by telling them that at school the next day, the girl sitting behind me asked if she could go to the nurse. When the teacher asked why, she said, "Someone back here has too much cologne on, and I'm about to throw up!" Okay, so I was probably more flammable than Michael Jackson's hair.

My young audience realizes that I have just taken a risk, and that means *I trusted them first.* When we lead our kids into an environment of trust like this, they will trust us and take our relationship deeper. Remember, today's teens want a relationship with us even more than we want a relationship with them.

Stories are a very nonconfrontational avenue of introducing ideas to young people. Teenagers will plug themselves into the characters and experience the story. When used at the right time, this is far more powerful than direct instruction (lecturing).

So what stories can you tell? We all have had life experiences that kids can connect with. One story I love to tell is about my dad. You see, for two decades my dad was an investigative reporter. In case you didn't grow up with a parent in the news business, let me give you some insight. My dad didn't know everything, but he could find the answer! As I recall, this particular evening was a weeknight like any other—with one exception. *The A-Team* was on television. I loved that show. My dad casually asked me, "Danny, did you do your math homework?" I answered, "Yep. Well, I didn't understand part of it, but I did what I knew." He offered to take a look at it. Now, my dad hadn't thought about that stuff for decades, and he looked baffled, reinforcing my wonderful excuse to see what Hannibal's plan would be this week. I resumed my position in front of the television and said, "Don't worry. I'll ask Mrs. Hoskins tomorrow." My dad had every confidence in Mrs. Hoskins. She was one of the best math teachers in our county.

What seemed like just seconds later, the doorbell rang. I heard someone talking and quickly recognized that voice. It was Mrs. Hoskins. She sat at the kitchen table—*my* kitchen table! With an open book in front her, she asked me what I was struggling with. Dumbfounded, I took the place next to her and stared blankly with my mouth open.

I was praying, *God, please help me get this so she'll leave. Please!* Somehow, with God's help, I faked my way through the private tutoring session. But the next day in math class, my sophomore nightmare came true. "Number thirteen? Anyone? Danny, I know you have this one right. We did it together last night at your house!" Sinking into my chair to try to hide my severe embarrassment, I had no rebuttal for the choir of my heckling peers.

I tell this story here for a couple of reasons. First, it's therapeutic for me. Talking about it helps me get over the trauma that still haunts me from the incident. Second, and more important, I want to show you where kids plug into that story. They automatically plug in to my character. I am showing them that I am "real." Unless we adults are real, they will not buy anything we say.

### Rousing

It's been said that you can teach anyone anything. All you have to do is capture that person's attention. When we are rousing with our teens, we will have their attention. That's why I often tell stories about choices I've made, and no story grabs kids' attention like the story about my abstinence pledge that I told in chapter 5. When I get to the part about my wedding night and giving my ring to Amanda, I can see the young women's hearts just melting. Why? They are plugging into my story. They want to be Amanda to a guy who cares that much about them. The story is rousing. Did I just tell them what to do? No. But do I have their attention? Yes. I do.

There are many techniques for being rousing, and I want to share two with you.

*Timing.* One day I was sitting in my office when a tall young man walked in, closed the door, and said, "Danny, will you do me a huge favor? Will you meet me at the mall tonight during my break?" He explained that he'd thought he could make a few bucks selling some marijuana, but halfway through the deal, things went bad, and his customer displayed a gun. He felt his life was in danger, and he didn't want to sit in the food court alone. I knew I couldn't do much to protect him in the mall, but I also knew I needed to capitalize on this teachable moment. I met him for his break, and we talked about his life and decisions he was making. With the threat of violence looming over him, it was the perfect time for me to help him examine his lifestyle.

The timing with your son or daughter may not be so dramatic. Did your daughter just find out about a friend who got pregnant? Did your son just see a boy banned from the baseball team because of alcohol or drug use? Did something happen in the media that has captured your teen's attention? Don't miss that golden opportunity when you find yourself with a captive audience.

*Listen and observe.* My wife amazes me. I'll be lying in bed next to my wife reading or relaxing, and almost from a dead sleep, she will say, "Danny, the dog needs to go out." I'm thinking, *We have a dog?* Yet she'd noticed something about his behavior that was a slight indicator of his need. If we can learn to listen to our kids with such fine-tuned ears, we will be much more strategically effective when we speak into their lives. One more thing. Would you rather give shotgun or rifle advice? A shotgun hits a large area with minimal penetration, but a rifle hits a specific target, even from a distance, with great impact. If we want our words to be rifle shots into the lives of our teenagers, we need to hear and understand them.

---

## TIPS FROM THE TRENCHES

*If you had to do your parenting over again, what would you do differently?*

S. Staples: We'd try to be more patient. We'd try to listen more. We'd worry less. We'd have faith that our best efforts were good enough and stop worrying about all of the other stuff.

C. Holland: I'd be more tolerant in disciplining them. I'd also give them less money and fewer things, gifts that made it harder for them to understand the work ethic.

R. Johnson: It's a miracle that any firstborn child turns out halfway decent! If I had to do it all over again, I wouldn't be nearly as uptight about the small stuff.

---

And here are ways we can listen better. First, we need to look beneath the surface and study our teens. The image teenagers project and who they really are can be very different things. So we need to look deeper than the outward appearance. *We need to study our teenagers to learn what makes them tick.*

A young woman came to my office one day and started to nervously make small talk. I didn't have any kind of relationship with this girl, but she was reaching out to me. So I began building a bridge into her life, and she responded by steering our relationship with her topics of conversation. She began to open up to me about a situation brewing between her and her father. At one point I specifically asked

> We were so scared that we were going to do it wrong that we never really relaxed. The older we got—and now with our youngest child—we're much more relaxed and deliberate about things.
>
> S. Johnson: Every single day we made an effort to do the best we could that day. I wish we could have taken more family vacations and spent more uninterrupted time with the kids.
>
> B. Waliszewski: I do wish I would have scheduled more special date nights with my children. A date night is something my wife and I practice (which has been really good for the kids to see modeled), but I've only rarely had those one-on-one dates with the kids. I should have done more!

her if he was abusing her, and she denied it. Several weeks later we talked again and she said, "Danny, I have to apologize to you. I lied to you. For the last nine years my father has raped me several times a week." I had simply paid attention to her and then worked to develop a relationship that could withstand the intensity of the pain she wanted to communicate to me.

Also key to listening well is *knowing our children's modes of communication*. Every one has a dominant personality type, and with each type comes unique strengths, weaknesses, and fears. Knowing these can make a huge difference in how effectively we communicate.

First, children with strong dominant personalities may struggle with authority, but they may also be unmovable when rooted in what they believe. Their fear of being used may mean they have trouble allowing others control over what they care about, but that same passion may later make them great leaders or visionaries. Second, kids who are natural verbal leaders and people-oriented extroverts may make friends easily, but they may struggle with their fear of social rejection more than introverted kids. This strength may later help them fulfill their purpose through public speaking, drama, music, or other creative expression, but this attribute could also make them more susceptible to pressure from friends to fit in. Third, our more stable kids who just want everyone to get along strive for predictable routine. Their greatest fear usually involves loss of security. They are peacemakers with more stable moods than many kids. Fourth, some of our kids are detail-oriented and more task- than people-oriented. They are often calculated and take care of their possessions. They may excel academically beyond their years and ask questions that require more detail than other kids their age. These kids usually fear criticism. Their fear may cause them to avoid trying new sports or other activities they believe they can't master quickly.

All of us have all four of these types, but we have two that are dominant. Personality study is not best suited for the detection of gifts and one's purpose, but rather the application of those gifts toward the fulfillment of that purpose. Knowing our kids' strengths and fears can help us package our communication in a way that can be best received.

When I was a teenager, I traveled with a team of other American teenagers to Mexico City. When we all arrived, we were briefed on what we should and should not do while communicating with the nationals. They told us, for instance, to not use the "okay" hand signal, because in Mexico it has the same meaning as the middle finger does in the U.S. Also, if we wanted someone to come to us, we needed to use the common hand motion with our palm down instead of palm up, which has sexual connotations for the Mexicans.

We all seemed to be paying attention with the exception of one of our leaders. After moving some of our equipment onto the service elevator, he instructed us to pile in. On the way down, the elevator stopped at a floor, the door opened, and a young woman who worked in housekeeping was standing there. "Come on in," Bob said as he motioned with his palm up. Seeing the five guys in the elevator, her eyes got wide, and she said, "No, gracias." Verbally and with both hands, Bob said "Okay," using the U.S. sign. I can assure you there wasn't a thought in Bob's head about making a sexual invitation to this young woman and then flipping her off after she declined. But when we expect our kids to communicate on our level, we are risking the same kind of misunderstanding. It is our responsibility as parents to communicate with our teens in ways they can understand.

In addition to knowing our kids and the way they communicate, *we need to compliment our teens and praise the effort they are showing in productive areas.* Your child or teenager will rise to your level of expectation. Complimenting is one way to instill dignity in your teens and to strengthen your relationship for input and discussion. And if you are looking for positive things to encourage, you will listen more closely to your teen's entire story, not just to the areas you want to discourage.

Fixating on the negative blips on our parental radar screens is unfortunately too easy. We must make an effort to find positive things our teens are doing that fly below the radar. When I want to connect with a teenager who is hurting, rebelling, or acting out, I study him to find the positive attribute that is masked behind his destructive behavior. For example, if other kids are imitating the destructive behavior or looking to him as a leader, I might tell that teenager, "You have a gift. You are a born leader. I can see you running a corporation some day." If the teenager is a student who is caught cheating, I might say to her, "This is not you. This is not the [insert name] I know. This incident will not be a defining moment of your life. I can see that you like to help others. I recently heard you giving good advice to [insert name], and I could tell that you really care. That's the kind of friend I would want at your age."

We need to encourage what we want to reproduce. Recently I caught a unique glimpse into the mind of my eight-year-old son. He was talking to my wife about a picture he was working on. "I love drawing pictures for Dad," he said. "Why?" Amanda asked. "Because I love it when he compliments me," he replied. Your seventeen-year-old may not articulate her feelings, but I can assure you that she feels the same way.

When we speak to the positive in our teenagers, recognizing their gifts and abilities, we feed them good food and they grow toward their purpose. If we create motivators for positive behavior, we reduce the need for our teenagers to try to capture our attention with negative behavior. We need to be artists painting elaborate scenes—the possibilities of what our kids can be—on the canvas of their imaginations for them to meditate on. These attractive potentialities then draw them to raise their expectations of themselves.

Finally, *we parents will listen better—and scale some walls on our relationship with our teens—if we ask them questions.* When you ask someone a question, you earn the right to be heard. When you value another's opinion, you earn the right to have your opinion considered in return. Asking your kids questions is also a powerful way to help them discover truth. They are still learning to discern right from wrong, a skill they need to be able to use when you are nowhere to be found. Teens are also figuring out where your information fits into their worldview, values, and life.

If we are serious about communicating with our kids, we need to be serious about speaking their language. We wouldn't think of going to France to communicate with the French without knowing their language. How much more should we be able to understand issues our kids are facing and then use those issues to improve our communication with them. This leads us into our third R.

## *Relevant*

Relevance is how we get past boredom. When information is relevant to us, it satisfactorily answers questions like these: *How does this apply to my life? How will this advice protect me? How will this help me understand my purpose? How will this help me achieve my dreams? What do I have to gain or lose? How will this keep me from pain and regrets?*

On the other hand, if information is too metaphorical, it becomes irrelevant to young people. If your words to describe what we put into our hearts and minds go something like this, "When a tree is planted near the water, its roots gather nutrients from this nearby source," you've lost them. You might have a great point, but if you can't make it relevant to their lives, it's worthless to them.

If your son, for example, hopes to reach a high rank in the armed forces or to become a law enforcement officer, any criminal arrest record would severely damage his dream, even to the point of ending it. Your "Stay away from drugs and wrong friends" instruction will be most relevant to your son when you demonstrate the connection between the ultimate consequences of this type of activity and the threat it poses to his dream.

This challenge to be relevant is especially important when we're talking with kids who choose to abuse drugs and alcohol. Remember, most drug use is slow suicide. Reasons for drug abusers to feel like they might succeed in life someday are nowhere to be found. So when we confront a teen about drug use, our information must be relevant. The successful commercials designed to stop teen smoking are founded on this principle. They often show cosmetic and social side effects of smoking rather than health effects that might be years down the road. Of course, there are bigger reasons for a young woman to stop smoking than *extra facial hair*, but those reasons are not as *relevant*. To address a young man's decision to smoke marijuana, we must also address attitudes behind the drug use. If you felt your life was nothing and never would be anything, why wouldn't you take something that makes you feel good at least for a while? If you had trouble talking to girls, why wouldn't you take Ecstasy to take the inhibitions away and make you feel confident?

## Relational

Again, nobody wants a family more than the kids who are inside your home and under your influence. And it is our responsibility as their parents to bridge any gap in the relationship. Everything about our teens might be screaming, "I don't want to hear this from you!" But we need to persist. We must passionately seek to understand our teens. Like a foreign nation, we must become fluent in "Millennial" so we are able to enter their arena and successfully communicate with them.

So how do you know if you have a good relationship with your son or daughter? Ask yourself this question: Can you waste time with them? No agenda. No goal. Just you and your teen. When you can waste time and simply enjoy your teen, you are developing a relationship with him or her. By the way, I've noticed that many of the moments I intend to be so special are not the ones I remember the most. The memories we seem to hold on to the longest are the ones we make along the way to the next event. We can plan many activities for our kids and buy them lots of toys, but there is something special about the times when we just sit down and connect with them. I am in no way implying that connecting is automatic. When we "waste" time with our teens, we need to do so in the environment they feel at home in.

## ENTER THEIR WORLD

As adults, we tend to see the young generation through the filter of our own personal experiences. Often we simply don't realize how different the world is for young people today. If we were foreigners seeking to connect with a completely different culture, though, we'd study their culture, language, religious idols, and anything else that's relevant. We'd learn what to say and what not to say. We would also tread lightly into their world; we would walk with the utmost cultural sensitivity. As foreigners, we would politely eat inedible, unpronounceable food that we would never touch at home, and we would conduct ourselves in a way that would minimize the obvious differences between their culture and ours. If we wanted to be received into their lives, we would not fly into their world as know-it-all-Westerners but as humble guests. Our effort to enter a foreign culture—like our teenager's environment—can communicate a powerful message about our respect and love.

Therefore, when it comes to the vital task of communicating life-saving and life-shaping information to our kids, we cannot be any less careful or passionate about successfully communicating with that "national" in the back bedroom than we would be with the national on the other side of the world. We cannot stand on the comfortable and safe soil of our land, yell commands from a distance, and expect life-changing results. We wouldn't expect that to be successful in any other cross-cultural setting. Why would we expect it to work in cross-cultural communication with our teenagers? When it comes to having an impact on your children and teens, remember this—and you've heard it before—there are no shortcuts.

Mentors, professional role models, and influential parents have to walk with teenagers in their environment. We cannot stay comfortably at a distance from the world they live in and still provide the leadership they want and need. We need to be creative and smart to reach our kids. What do your kids like to do? Do it with them. Where do they like to eat? Eat there with them. What movies would they like to see? Go to the theater with them. My sons are constantly asking me to play with them. "Daddy, play basketball with me." "Dad, can I help you on the computer?" They are asking me to connect with them in their environment. I am a wise parent if I find the place we can waste time together and then invest my energy and resources there.

## 10

# Passing On Your Legacy: Maximizing the Effectiveness of Your Relationship

Since each of our families is unique, the principles of developing relationships and raising teenagers are likely to look vastly different from home to home. It is desperation that drives us outside our comfortable walls and our preconceived boxes. To make the most of our season of influence in our teens' lives, there are some things we need to consider.

### DIFFERENT IS DIFFERENT, NOT WRONG

"His grandfather was a Marine, I was a Marine, and someday Tommy will be a Marine." From my conversation with this father, I got the impression that he wasn't too inspired by his son's theatrical skills. Tommy was indeed a gifted actor with a heart of innocence, but he followed the course expected of him, turned his back on his gifts, and became a soldier. Now, my father-in-law is a retired Marine, and I have tremendous respect for those who fight for our country, but I also realize that not every child born to a soldier is gifted to be a soldier.

But I also realize how powerful a father's dream for his son can be. With a public Ivy League school in my backyard, I have the opportunity to visit the College of William and Mary almost every week. Since my wife is pursuing her master's degree there, I will often visit the bookstore with her. It is packed with promotional gear for everyone from birth on up. As much as I would love for my boys to attend a university as great as William and Mary, I must put aside my preferences, allow them to discover their uniqueness, and equip them to achieve their purpose.

As parents, though, we often assume that we know what is best for our kids, and we—and they—become ensnared in the expectation trap. Often we parents are motivated by the desire to gain approval from our own parents, the neighbors, friends at church, or co-workers. In our pursuit of approval, our children can be forced into boxes they were never designed to be in, and the result is great frustration and conflict in the home. If we parents aren't careful, our personal agendas can overpower the authentic purposes our children were created to fulfill.

Several years ago, for example, a beauty-pageant director who attended my church asked me to help her by being a judge. It seemed like a unique opportunity, so I agreed. Countless little girls walked—

or were carried—across the stage. I have to admit that I was shocked by the passion of the mothers, and they were probably shocked by my lack of attention to the details they had invested so much energy in. All the little girls looked cute to me. I tried to be objective and honest without crushing any little self-esteems. Little did I know that it wasn't the little esteems I should have been most concerned about. It was the big ones! I was bombarded with parents screaming at me as if I had just fired them from twenty-year careers. "Why did she get a four and not a five? What! Are you blind?" I was caught in a tornado of pure, unbridled parental passion!

When passion like that is directed at launching our kids into *their* purpose, our kids will recognize the ally they have in us and rely on our passion to fuel their lives.

## MIXED SIGNALS

As you try to establish a stronger relationship with your teenager, you may notice that you'll get some mixed signals. It's not uncommon for kids to balk at new boundaries or put forth an image that doesn't match who they really are. They are thinking, *If someone rejects me, it's okay because that's not the real me.* They desperately want someone to break through the smoke screen of protection that surrounds them.

Several years ago I worked with a fourteen-year-old girl who was struggling with some serious issues. One night I was notified that she was suicidal and missing from her home. By the time I got there, law enforcement officers and the fire department were combing the area in search of her. As I entered the girl's house, I noticed family pictures everywhere. I was shocked, however, because there were lots of pictures of Mom, Dad, and two siblings, but the young woman we were searching for wasn't in any of the family pictures. I asked the mother where the girl's father was. She answered, "He's upstairs in bed. He refuses to get up and look for her." The mother went on to explain that fourteen years before, someone of a different race had raped her. She got pregnant and, against her husband's wishes, kept her daughter. That young girl may say that she hates her father, but deep inside she is crying out, *Dad, please wake up and search for me. I know I represent something painful, but I need to be loved.*

## TIPS FROM THE TRENCHES

*What did you do to balance your time between your vocation and your family?*

S. Staples: We found some common shared time that we could *all* regularly fit into our schedules (dinnertime, for example).

T. Baehr: By God's grace and by involving my four children in most of what I did.

C. Holland: Prioritize. At times I even left work early to be a part of [my kids'] lives. [I] also chose to do things with the kids that may not have been my first choice.

R. Johnson: I've heard people say that it's not the quantity of time but the quality of time that matters. That's not true. The people in your family spell love T-I-M-E. You

In *Every Child Can Succeed,* Cynthia Tobias writes, "The quality of the relationship you have with each child will determine the effectiveness of the techniques you use. If you have cultivated a loving and healthy relationship with each of your children, they will care very much about preserving it. If there is no benefit in keeping the parental relationship intact, your efforts to discipline and motivate may have little or no effect. Even the child with the strongest will responds more to love and genuine kindness than to creative or flashy methods and approaches."[1]

James was a seventeen-year-old sophomore who transferred from a large inner-city school to a rural one. He behaved aggressively,

> may not always be able to do a whole lot, but I think if you have a set mealtime and come around your table, that goes a long way.... I didn't look at just the quality of time I spent [with my kids], but how much time. That's what my kids were crying out for. I also learned to turn off my cell phone when I was spending time with them.
>
> S. Johnson: I prayed that God would take up the slack between what we gave our boys and what they needed to get from us. God's mercy was there. Sunday lunch was a great time for our family. So was Saturday breakfast. Many of our special time centers around food. Sometimes we are up late at night talking. You have to be available when they want to talk.

particularly in math class. His outbursts became a recurring problem. What nobody knew was that James had only first-grade math knowledge. I am convinced that the behavior James displayed in class was his way of protecting himself from potential ridicule should his lack of knowledge be revealed. James was in survival mode, protecting his dignity at any cost.

People often hide behind such smoke screens to protect themselves from rejection. While projecting a negative image, inside they tell themselves, *It's okay if they don't like me. You and I know this is not the real me.* For a teenager, security seems more likely with the "real me" hidden. But as soon as parents and caring adults start safely handling the "fake me," the teen will seek opportunities to test us further until she realizes she can trust us with the "real me" she desperately desires to reveal. So be on the alert for these mixed signals and capitalize on them. Time and tenacity will help produce the trust you need to take your relationship with your teen to the next level.

## FOUR IMPORTANT TASKS

Not only do your teens want you in their lives, but they also need you in their lives. As lazy as they may seem, your teenagers are actually working very hard during these years to accomplish four difficult life tasks. They can no more accomplish these tasks with you in total control of their lives than they can learn to drive a car from the passenger seat. But you can offer guidance and help them succeed.

So what are these four tasks? First, our teenagers are working at identifying their life's purpose. That purpose will give them a sense of significance and help them gain independence. Their vocations will also meet their need for self-esteem.

Second, while attempting to navigate into the deep waters of determining their purpose, they are also trying to internalize the values we have imparted to them and make them their own. This process helps them become people of integrity. Establishing values will meet their self-esteem need to have their own experiences. This idea is truest when it comes to a young person's spirituality. Our kids don't want our faith because we had an experience years ago. They want to have their own experience and build their own faith upon it. As an influential parent, we can create opportunities for our children to have their own experiences. We can take a mission trip to a foreign country with them or participate with them in the church musical— you get the idea. When they watch Mom and Dad do ministry and share in it at their own level, they take ownership of their faith and build bonds with us. By providing these experiences for them, we make it easy for them to own what we have grown to value.

Third, our teenagers are developing their social identities, and that means dealing with powerful sexual feelings. With an established social identity comes a sense of community and belonging.

Fourth, teenagers are discovering their uniqueness as their identities emerge. They are trying to find a place in life to call their own. The goal for them is to move from being externally supported by us to internally supporting themselves. Once they're living according to solid principles, they will gain a tremendous feeling of inner confidence. Clearly, even if your sleep-until-noon teens don't seem to possess your work ethic, they are very active and in need of your guidance.

## PICK YOUR BATTLES; WIN THE WAR

With these tasks in mind, we can see that in a few short years, many vital things must be accomplished. As protective and necessary as rules are, it is important for parents to make what matters most, matter most. In other words, it's not as important for us to win each battle as it is to win the war. The boundaries we consistently maintain protect our teenagers from some risks but not all of them. Think back to the guardrail analogy. Occasionally drivers do very stupid things, so the guardrail doesn't offer the protection they need. The same holds true for our teenagers. Nevertheless, we parents do what we can to help them make right choices and protect their future. We should not micromanage them to the point where they are not able to practice making choices as individuals. The perfect time for our teens to learn how to make those choices is when we are standing next to them, helping as needed.

On the other hand, when we intervene and keep our kids from experiencing the consequences of their actions, we rob them of character development. Protecting our teenagers from the consequences of their actions may help us feel as if we are winning a battle for them, but in reality we are enabling them to continue to develop destructive habits in their lives. Let me give you an example. Jason is a star athlete in his senior year of high school. Lacking better judgment, Jason decides to show up at a school function intoxicated. When confronted by school personnel and law enforcement, Jason decides to make a break for the door and run from them. After a dangerous pursuit and a physical struggle, the police arrest Jason.

Jason's mom and dad are not pleased with his decision to use alcohol at an early age, and they are even more disappointed at the repercussions this will have on his high-school athletic career and possible scholarship hopes. So they decide to challenge the school administrator's actions and school district's policy. If Mom and Dad succeed and see Jason return to athletics, they may have won a battle. But in the scope of Jason's growth and his character development, that victory may cost them the war. No matter what Mom and Dad tell Jason, they have just trained him to avoid consequences at any cost. They can tell him all day long that they are disappointed that he ran from the police, but they trained him to do just that: escape consequences.

Clearly, we parents need to remember to major in the majors and minor in the minors. Our mind-set must be to win the overall war. When we take our focus off that ultimate goal, our parenting can be easily shaken by sporadic behavior. Furthermore, when boundaries are in place to protect our teenagers from bad choices and serious negative consequences, we have the freedom to come alongside them, influence them as they confront minor challenges, and teach them how to maneuver through disappointment, hardship, and difficulty.

Too often, however, minor issues become more an issue of control. Tobias writes, "It's difficult to maintain a positive and loving relationship with your [strong-willed child] if the two of you are constantly battling for control." She goes on to offer this guideline: "In our home, there are certain nonnegotiable issues: (1) physical safety, e.g., we don't walk in front of moving cars or ride without seat belts, and (2) moral and spiritual values, e.g., we don't lie or hurt others. Beyond those, we try to let our [strong-willed child] negotiate to a certain extent."[2]

## TEENS HAVE LOTS OF FRIENDS; BE A PARENT

She was fourteen years old but looked like she was twenty. Her mother noticed that she was getting more and more physical with the guys she was developing relationships with. Red flags were everywhere. But her mother, a devout Christian, responded with, "I don't want to push her away, so I'll just pray for her." This mother wanted to be her daughter's friend. Your son and daughter may have many friends, but you are their only parents. And parents can effectively maintain a positive relationship with their teenagers even while disciplining them.

I am reminded of a divorced father who wanted to be close to his son, who was living with his mother. So Dad convinced his son that living with him would be much more fun than living with his mother. Dad threw a party for many of his son's friends. At the party were thirty teenagers and more than two hundred open containers of alcohol. When law enforcement officers broke up the party, the dad was charged with nine counts of contributing to the delinquency of a minor. This boy's father ended up serving six years in jail for his crimes. He lost his career, house, cars, boat, and, most important, his son.

## DON'T BE A DROPOUT PARENT

Between the ages of fourteen and twenty-four, teenagers and emerging adults make the most important decisions of their lives, decisions such as whom they will marry, how educated they will be, and what their vocation will be. During this season, then, it's vital that we parents do not fade away. A national youth speaker, for example, conducted a parent night and invited all parents from all the high schools in the district. Nearly four thousand parents were notified, but fewer than thirty parents attended. The drop-in attendance at high-school PTA meetings as compared to elementary-school PTA meetings was shocking. Fewer and fewer parents are involved in the lives of their teenagers.

Many parents express to me that they are very busy trying to maintain the lifestyle that their teens enjoy. Also, between the teens' schedule and the parents' schedule, there are fewer hours available to connect. Many parents give their teenagers credit cards and other material goods to compensate for the lack of time spent with them. Yet experts agree that one of the single biggest mistakes a well-meaning parent can make is providing their kids with too much stuff. But the fact is, teenagers today have more disposable income than any other age group.[3] Many young people are growing up without limits, learning that others are responsible for fulfilling all their cravings, and thinking that they are entitled to many luxuries. Kids don't need stuff; kids need parents.

In fact, our teenage kids need us as much as they have ever needed us. They need us, for instance, to draw out potential they don't recognize in themselves or cannot access alone. We are able to see things in them that they are unable to see for themselves. In the battle for their future, our kids also need to know that we are warriors fighting by their sides. We need to draw our parental sword and say, "I will protect your purity, I will protect your potential, and I will fight for you." When we commit our lives to our teens in this way, they will recognize us as powerful allies. Remember, long after you are gone, the greatest impact of your life will be seen in the lives of those you have trained.

"Waste time with me." That's what our kids are asking us to do. When we take the time to invest in their lives, we will not be disappointed. A focus group of ninety-five-year-olds was asked to complete the statement, "If I had it to do all over again, I would..." Their top three answers were:

1. I would spend more time in reflection.

2. I would risk more.

3. I would invest my time in things that really matter.[4]

These are powerful statements from individuals approaching the end of their lives. We also need to realize that the loudest voices in our busy adult world may not be the most significant or profitable in the long-term scope of our teens' lives. We need to decide to live our lives so we'll have no regrets.

## SMILE, YOU'RE ON CANDID CAMERA

Robert Fulghum, author of *All I Really Need to Know I Learned in Kindergarten,* said, "Do not worry that your children never listen to you; worry that they are always *watching* you." The truth is, our kids are learning from us every waking moment we're with them. That isn't completely bad news. When we embrace the fact that we are shaping our children by the example of our behavior even when we are not teaching them with our words, we recognize the very powerful tool we have in our possession. When we take care of our bodies, reduce our personal debt, and give priority to spiritual development, we are teaching our children that these things are important.

Neither the perfect parent nor the perfect child exists. You may find yourself in a family that could easily be labeled dysfunctional. Yet if you are imperfect, like me, you will be happy to know that properly handling our struggles in front of our teenagers gives them powerful examples of how to deal with difficulty. When our kids grow up watching occasional marital conflict being resolved without anyone leaving the relationship, they are trained in what to do when conflict arises in their own lives. When our kids grow up watching us struggle financially and go through difficult times, they learn that a family can enjoy each other without all the material comforts in life. When they watch their father be angry without becoming violent, throwing things, or hitting others, they learn how to deal with their own anger. And watching their father take the risk of leaving his job to pursue his life's purpose teaches them about the value of pursuing purpose and growing up in their uniqueness. Whenever we handle ourselves with character and integrity in difficult times, class is in session, and the students are giving us their undivided attention.

# CONCLUSION

Every morning each one of us wakes up to a family setting that is unique and, for most of us, less than perfect. As extended families unify in purpose and relationally influence the children and teenagers in their homes, their blended experiences, gifts, talents, and vision can come together to launch the next generation to a level they themselves never attained. As life coaches, each adult in the family needs to see the potential inside their teenagers and encourage them to achieve things they might not imagine on their own. Like a warrior bent on changing the face of a nation, we precisely and skillfully launch our teenagers into adulthood to make their mark in this world. We must never lose sight of the task at hand. We must continually see potential, gifts, and purpose through our foresight. And no matter how hard that teenager makes you work to establish and preserve your relationship, always look beyond the behavior to the value and unique purpose deep within.

But many gifts are wasted. That's why it's been said that the most valuable soil in the world—more valuable than the diamond mines of Venezuela, the oil fields of Iraq, or the gold in Fort Knox—is the graveyard. As I sit on the edge of an auditorium stage and look out over the thousand teenagers filing in, I can't help but wonder how many of them will take with them to the grave what they have been given to contribute to the world. How many great artists and poets have been buried with their gifts? Is the cure for cancer inside a young dreamer whose dream is being crushed early? I spend my life doing what I do to keep such riches from being buried in a graveyard. I want to finish my life having done absolutely everything I was put here to accomplish.

I encourage you as parents—as professional role models, coaches, and mentors—to do your part to help your teens discover and use the gifts they've been given. Too many people who have gone before them died having never used their gifts and having never left their mark.

I encourage you to make a difference in the life of a young person every day. And I leave you with the reminder that hangs on my study wall: "A hundred years from now it will not matter what my bank account was, the sort of house I lived in, or the kind of car I drove...but the world may be different because I was important in the life of a child."

Go make a difference.

# NOTES

## Chapter 1

1. Paul Rogat Loeb, *Generation at the Crossroads: Apathy and Action on the American Campus* (New Brunswick, NJ: Rutgers University, 1994), 51.

2. Dawson McAllister and Pat Springle, *Saving the Millennial Generation: New Ways to Reach the Kids You Care About in These Uncertain Times* (Nashville: Nelson, 1999), 5.

## Chapter 2

1. Tim Celek and Dieter Zander, *Inside the Soul of a New Generation: Insight and Strategies for Reaching Busters* (Grand Rapids: Zondervan, 1996), 32.

## Chapter 3

1. Theodore Baehr, *So You Want to Be in Pictures? A Christian Resource for "Making It" in Hollywood* (Nashville: Broadman and Holman, 2005), 80.

2. Paul Johnson, *Modern Times: The World from the Twenties to the Nineties,* rev. ed. (New York: HarperPerennial, 1992), 130.

3. Mike Murdock, *The Assignment: Powerful Secrets for Discovering Your Destiny* (Tulsa, OK: Albury, 1997), 35–36.

4. Donald F. Roberts, PhD, and others, "Generation M: Media in the Lives of 8-18 Year-Olds," A Kaiser Family Foundation Study, Program for the Study of Entertainment Media and Health no. 7251, March 2005, http://www.kff.org/entmedia/7251.cfm.

5. Linda L. Creighton, "A New World Apart: Mysteries of the Teen Years," *U.S. News and World Report Special Edition* (2005), 23–24.

6. Phil Phillips, *Saturday Morning Mind Control* (Nashville: Oliver-Nelson, 1991), 54, quoted in Dave Grossman and Gloria DeGaetano, *Stop Teaching Our Kids to Kill: A Call to Action Against TV* (NY: Crown, 1999), 26.

7. Aletha C. Huston and others, *Big World, Small Screen: The Role of Television in American Society* (Lincoln: University of Nebraska, 1992), 136, quoted in Grossman and DeGaetano, *Stop Teaching Our Kids to Kill*, 34–35.

8. Chris J. Boyatzis, "Of Power Rangers and V-Chips," *Young Children*, vol. 52, no. 7 (November 1997), 75, quoted in Grossman and DeGaetano, *Stop Teaching Our Kids to Kill*.

9. "Does Watching Sex on Television Influence Teens' Sexual Activity?" Rand Corporation, 2004, www.rand.org/pubs/research_briefs/RB9068/index1.html.

10. "It's Just Harmless Entertainment," Parents Television Council Publications, 2005, www.parentstv.org/ptc/facts/mediafacts.asp.

11. Internet Filter Reviews 2006, "Pornography Industry Revenue Statistics," http://internet-filter-review.toptenreviews.com/

internet-pornography-statistics.html; Jerry Ropelato, "Internet Pornography Statistics."

12. Roberts, PhD, and others, "Generation M."

13. Koren Zailckas, *Smashed: Story of a Drunken Girlhood* (New York: Penguin, 2005), 17.

## Chapter 4

1. Kevin N. Wright and Karen E. Wright, "Family Life and Delinquency and Crime: A Policymaker's Guide to the Literature"; see references to Ann Goetting, "Patterns of Homicide Among Children," *Criminal Justice and Behavior* 16 (1989): 63–80, and Jill Leslie Rosenbaum, "Family Dysfunction and Female Delinquency," *Crime and Delinquency* 35, no. 1 (1989): 31–44.

2. Patrick F. Fagan, "The Real Root Causes of Violent Crime: The Breakdown of Marriage, Family, and Community," *Making America Safer: What Citizens and Their State and Local Officials Can Do to Combat Crime,* ed. Edwin Meese III and Robert E. Moffit (Washington DC: Heritage Foundation, 1997), 3.

3. Fagan, *Making America Safer,* 4.

4. Fagan, *Making America Safer,* 3.

5. Jennifer L. White and others, "How Nearly Can We Tell? Predictors of Childhood Conduct Disorder and Adolescent Delinquency," *Criminology* 28, no. 4 (1990): 507–33.

6. Kevin N. Wright and Karen E. Wright, "Family Life and Delinquency and Crime: A Policymaker's Guide to the

Literature," prepared under interagency agreement between the Office of Juvenile Justice and Delinquency Prevention and the Bureau of Justice Assistance of the U.S. Department of Justice (1992): 11.

7. Rolf Loeber and Magda Stouthamer-Loeber, "Development and Risk Factors of Juvenile Antisocial Behavior and Delinquency" and "Family Factors as Correlates and Predictors of Juvenile Conduct Problems and Delinquency," ed. M. Tonry and N. Morris, *Crime and Justice: An Annual Review of Research* 7 (Chicago: University of Chicago, 1986), 29–149.

8. "Family Status of Delinquents in Juvenile Correctional Facilities in Wisconsin," Division of Youth Services, Wisconsin Department of Health and Family Services, April 1994, reported in *The Family in America,* Rockford Institute.

9. D. O. Lewis and others, "Neuropsychiatric, Psychoeducational and Family Characteristics of 14 Juveniles Condemned to Death in the United States," *American Journal of Psychiatry* 145 (1988): 585–89.

10. "America's Children: Key National Indicators of Well-Being 2001," Federal Interagency Forum on Child and Family Statistics, Washington DC.

11. Jason Fields, "America's Families and Living Arrangements: March 2000," *Current Population Reports,* U.S. Census Bureau, Washington DC, P20–537.

12. Tavia Simmons and Grace O'Neill, Households and Families: 2000, *Current Population Reports,* U.S. Census Bureau, Washington DC, P20–537.

13. Fields, "Arrangements," P20–537.

14. T. D. Jakes, *The Great Investment: Faith, Family and Finance to Build a Rich Spiritual Life* (New York: Putman, 2000), 78.

15. Ellen Galinsky, *Ask the Children: What America's Children Really Think about Working Parents* (New York: William Morrow, 1999).

16. Claudia Wallis, "The Kids Are Alright," *Time,* July 5, 1999.

17. Koren Zailckas, *Smashed: Story of a Drunken Girlhood* (New York: Penguin, 2005), 12–13.

18. Neil Howe and William Strauss, *Millennials Rising: The Next Great Generation* (New York: Vintage, 2000), 202.

## Chapter 5

1. John Wooden and Steve Jamison, *Wooden on Leadership* (New York: McGraw-Hill, 2005), 80.

2. Pat Robertson and Bob Slosser, *The Secret Kingdom* (Nashville: Nelson, 1987), 161–62.

3. "Passing the Baton," a live training presentation developed by Dr. Jeff Myers, www.myersinstitute.com.

4. Stephen R. Covey, *The Seven Habits of Highly Effective Families* (New York: Golden Books, 1997), 72.

5. Stephen R. Covey, *The Seven Habits of Highly Effective People* (New York: Free Press, 2004), 98.

## Chapter 6

1. Morris Massey, *The People Puzzle: Understanding Yourself and Others* (Reston, VA: Reston, 1979).

2. Tim Kimmel, *Why Christian Kids Rebel: Trading Heartache for Hope* (Nashville: W Publishing, 2004), 200.

## Chapter 7

1. "Passing the Baton," a live training presentation developed by Dr. Jeff Myers, www.myersinstitute.com.
2. James Dobson, *The Strong-Willed Child* (Carol Stream, IL: Tyndale, 1978), 99.

## Chapter 8

1. S. A. Sanders and J. M. Reinisch, "Would You Say You 'Had Sex' If…?" *Journal of the American Medical Association* 281, no. 3 (1999): 275–77.
2. P. F. Horan, J. Phillips, and N. E. Hagan, "The Meaning of Abstinence for College Students," *Journal of HIV/AIDS Prevention and Education for Adolescents and Children* 2, no. 2 (1998): 51–66.
3. F. L. Sonenstein and others, "Changes in Sexual Behavior and Condom Use Among Teenaged Males: 1988 to 1995," *American Journal of Public Health* 88, no. 6 (1988): 956–59; J. Abma and others, "Fertility, Family Planning, and Women's Health: New Data from The 1995 National Survey of Family Growth, *Vital and Health Statistics* 23, no. 19 (1997); and E. O. Laumann and others, *National Health and Social Life Survey,* 1992, Chicago and Ann Arbor: National Opinion Research Center and Inter-University Consortium for Political and Social Research, 1995.

4. Stenzel, *No Screwin' Around* (DVD), 2005, www.pam stenzel.com.

5. Stenzel, *No Screwin' Around*.

6. Stenzel, *No Screwin' Around*.

7. Stenzel, *No Screwin' Around*.

8. "Remarks by Dr. Henry Foster, Nominee for U.S. Surgeon General," School of Public Health, George Washington University, The White House Office of the Press Secretary, February 10, 1995, press release, www.ibiblio.org/pub/archives/whitehouse-papers/1995/Feb/1995-02-10-foster-remarks-at-george-washington-u-as-prepared.text.

9. "Abstinence Clearinghouse Fact Sheet on Human Papilloma Virus," The Abstinence Clearinghouse, www.abstinence.net, quoted in Josh McDowell, *Why True Love Waits: A Definitive Book on How to Help Your Youth Resist Sexual Pressure* (Carol Stream, IL: Tyndale, 2002), 233.

10. Josh McDowell and Dick Day, *Why Wait? What You Need to Know about the Teen Sexuality Crisis* (San Bernardino, CA: Here's Life, 1987), 79.

11. "Pornography Industry Revenue Statistics," Internet Filter Reviews 2006, http://internet-filter-review.toptenreviews.com/internet-pornography-statistics.html.

12. Family Safe Media, Nextphase Inc. d.b.a. Family Safe Media, 1998–2006, www.familysafemedia.com/pornography_statistics.html.

13. *The Southern Poverty Law Center's Intelligence Report* 114, Summer 2004, 13 (sidebar).

14. "One in Seven Teen Video Game Players is Addicted," April 24, 2003, National Institute on Media and the Family, www.mediafamily.org/press/20030424-2.shtml.

15. David Walsh, PhD, and others, "MediaWise Video Game Report Card," December 19, 2002, National Institute on Media and the Family, www.mediafamily.org/research/report_vgrc_2002-2.shtml.

16. Rebecca L. Collins and others, "Watching Sex on Television Predicts Adolescent Initiation of Sexual Behavior," *Pediatrics,* vol. 114, no. 3, September 2004.

17. These tips have been adapted from "Smart Guide to Kid's TV," American Academy of Pediatrics, www.aap.org/family/smarttv.htm.

18. U.S. Department of Justice, Bureau of Justice Statistics, *Drug and Crime Facts,* www.ojp.usdoj.gov/bjs/dcf/du.htm.

19. L. D. Johnston and others, *Monitoring the Future: National Results on Adolescent Drug Use: Overview of Key Findings, 2002* (Bethesda, MD: National Institute on Drug Abuse, 2003).

20. "Research on the Nature and Extent of Drug Use in the United States" *Drug Abuse and Addiction Research, The Sixth Triennial Report to Congress,* National Institute on Drug Abuse, www.drugabuse.gov/STRC/Forms.html.

21. "The Surgeon General's Call to Action to Prevent Suicide," U.S. Public Health Services, Department of Health and Human Services, 1999, www.infoline.org/Crisis/warning signs.asp.

22. Ted Haggard and John Bolin, *Confident Parents, Exceptional Teens* (Grand Rapids: Zondervan, 1999), 58.

## Chapter 9

1. Lionel Dahmer, *A Father's Story* (New York: William Morrow, 1994), 60.
2. Tim Celek and Dieter Zander, *Inside the Soul of a New Generation* (Grand Rapids: Zondervan, 1996), 100–108.

## Chapter 10

1. Cynthia Ulrich Tobias, *Every Child Can Succeed: Making the Most of Your Child's Learning Style* (Colorado Springs: Focus on the Family, 1996), preface.
2. Cynthia Ulrich Tobias, *You Can't Make Me (But I Can Be Persuaded): Strategies for Bringing Out the Best in Your Strong-Willed Child* (Colorado Springs: WaterBrook, 1999), 27–28
3. Katy Kelly, "Stuff Makes the Teen," *U.S. News and World Report Special Edition* (2005), 58.
4. Tony Campolo, *Who Switched the Price Tags* (Nashville, W Publishing, 1986), quoted in "Passing the Baton," a live training presentation developed by Dr. Jeff Myers, www.myersinstitute.com.

# About the Author

DANNY HOLLAND has studied youth culture professionally for nearly two decades and has traveled across the nation and around the world speaking to hundreds of thousands of people. As the president and founder of Parent and Teen Universities Inc.—P-T-U.org—he teaches parents, educators, ministers, and others how to better understand and connect with this young generation. When Danny isn't speaking to adults, he can be found speaking to students, helping them embrace their purpose and avoid regrets. He and his wife, Amanda, have two sons. You can learn more about Danny's work by visiting DannyHolland.com.

For more information on how you can reach teens,
please visit ReachingTeens.com.